BEADS
OF
HEALING

PRAYER, TRAUMA, AND
SPIRITUAL WHOLENESS

KRISTEN E. VINCENT

UPPER
ROOM BOOKS®
NASHVILLE

BEADS OF HEALING
Prayer, Trauma, and Spiritual Wholeness
© 2016 by Kristen E. Vincent
All rights reserved.

UPPER ROOM®, UPPER ROOM BOOKS® and design logos are trademarks owned by THE UPPER ROOM®, Nashville, Tennessee. All rights reserved.

Upper Room Books website: books.upperroom.org
Cover design: Bruce Gore | GoreStudio.com
Cover photo: Kristen E. Vincent
Author photo: Gerald Patrick Photography

At the time of publication all websites referenced in this book were valid. However, due to the fluid nature of the internet some addresses may have changed, or the content may no longer be relevant.

Scripture quotations not otherwise identified are from the Common English Bible. Copyright © 2011 Common English Bible. Used by permission.

All scripture designated ESV are from The Holy Bible, English Standard Version® (ESV®), copyright © 2001 by Crossway, a publishing ministry of Good News Publishers. Used by permission. All rights reserved.

All scripture designated (NIV) are taken from the Holy Bible, New International Version®. NIV® Copyright ©1973, 1978, 1984, 2011 by Biblica, Inc.® Used by permission. All rights reserved worldwide.

Scripture passages designated NRSV are taken from the New Revised Standard Version Bible © 1989, Division of Christian Education of the National Council of the Churches of Christ in the United States of America. Used by permission. All rights reserved.

The excerpt from LIVING PRAYER by Robert Benson, copyright © 1998 by Robert Benson. Used by permission of Tarcher, an imprint of Penguin Publishing Group, a division of Penguin Random House LLC.

LIBRARY OF CONGRESS CATALOGING-IN-PUBLICATION DATA
Names: Vincent, Kristen E., author.
Title: Beads of healing : prayer, trauma, and spiritual wholeness / Kristen E. Vincent.
Description: Nashville, TN : Upper Room Books, [2016]
Identifiers: LCCN 2016029263 | ISBN 9780835816359 (print) | ISBN 9780835816366 (mobi) | ISBN 9780835816373 (epub)
Subjects: LCSH: Spiritual healing. | Healing--Religious aspects—Christianity. | Post-traumatic stress disorder--Religious aspects—Christianity. | Pain--Religious aspects—Christianity. | Prayer—Christianity. | Beads--Religious aspects—Christianity.
Classification: LCC BT732.5 .V56 2016 | DDC 248.8/6--dc23
LC record available at https://lccn.loc.gov/2016029263

To The Academy for Spiritual Formation,
especially the leadership and members of Academy #34.
This is our story.

To my mom. This is our story.

To my fellow trauma survivors. This is our story.

Me (age 7) and my brother, Tyler

Frederick Buechner once said, "To be a writer, one must be a good steward of their pain." I think that is true as well for those who would pray. To be such a steward creates the possibility that others might be healed by your witness to such a thing, that others might see the mercies granted to you in your suffering as evidence of the compassion of God for those who are broken. This gift of our brokenness is often the only gift that we can give or receive with any real honesty and with any real hope and with any real power.

—Robert Benson, *Living Prayer*

CONTENTS

INTRODUCTION

Some of you know me from my work with prayer beads. It's been one of the greatest joys of my journey here on earth, leading to incredible experiences, profound testimonies, new relationships, exciting opportunities. But there is more to the prayer bead story. The prayer beads are actually part of a larger story of my journey of healing. If you understand this part of my story, you will have a greater appreciation for the gift of the prayer beads.

This book records my journey of healing from trauma. You will read about profound pain and terror, particularly at the beginning of the book. I think it's important you know that up front. If you have any moments of pain in your life—and who of us doesn't—my story may bring up certain feelings or memories for you. Try not to judge them or fear them. It will get better. That's the point of this book. It is a story of hope.

Merriam-Webster's defines trauma as a deeply distressing or disturbing experience that can cause a person to have mental or emotional problems "for a very long time." That pretty much sums up my experience. My traumatic event took place when I was seven. As I write this, I am forty-eight years old. My husband will be the first to attest to the many sleep disturbances I have had throughout our twenty-plus years together. Until recently, the fear and pain of that long-ago event remained a constant in my life. What really got my attention, though, was this little factoid buried within the definition: the word *trauma* derives from the Greek word *trauma*, which means "wound." This little word's cousin is the Greek word *tetrainein*, which means "to pierce."

That makes sense to me. When we experience any type of trauma—whether violence, disaster, betrayal, death of a loved one—there may or may not be physical damage and there are varying levels of emotional damage. But it's a sure thing, always and everywhere, that we experience *spiritual* damage. The shock and pain of the event pierces our hearts, that central place where we first encountered God's love and from which all else flows, leaving a wound from which pours our deepest pain. At first glance we tend to associate that pain with the people or situations that were relevant to the traumatic event. Digging deeper, however, we begin to unearth spiritual pain, pain that focuses on God. We begin to believe that God has betrayed us, punished us, or abandoned us. We feel sorrow, anger, or despair. We wonder whether we can share our emotions with God. We wonder whether we can trust God.

Because this pain is so deep and so profound, we may not even know it's there. We may go to church, pray, get involved in service projects, or meet with others who share our faith. Then over days, weeks, or years, our spiritual life changes. We find that we are spending less time going to church, praying, or joining in mission. We find reasons to avoid meeting with others who share our faith. We question, silently or aloud, whether God hears our prayers. People ask about the change, and we can't quite figure it out. Left untended, this wound in our heart festers and grows until one day we find ourselves alone and afraid in the wilderness.

This book begins with the event that traumatized me, piercing the place where I had once known I was deeply loved by God. It follows my journey of pain and doubt, fear and betrayal, of a diagnosis of Post-Traumatic Stress Disorder (PTSD), and the path that finally led to hope and the healing of that terrible, inner spiritual wound. In the words of Nadia Bolz-Weber, I am writing from my scars rather than my wounds. In short, I am writing as one who knows from the very core of my being that I am and have always been deeply loved by God. I have recovered my truth.

This is my true story. It may be yours too. Whether the characteristics of our traumatic events and journey resemble one another or not, we share many of the same symptoms. As my friend Paul says, "Pain is pain." And we all long for healing, for a life that is full and extravagant and no longer shadowed by our trauma. We yearn to know God's deep love for us. Hence, this book.

This is my true story of healing. Sister Kathleen Flood, one of my favorite people, says that when we tell our stories of healing, we help others share their stories of healing as well. Better yet, when we share our stories of healing, we form a deeper, truer understanding of God—a patchwork of our various experiences, journeys, and interpretations. I offer this book with the abundant, wildly unabashed hope that it may help you in your healing process. Then you too can share your story of healing, and together we can witness the unfolding glory of God's perfect grace.

My story of healing centers primarily around my participation in The Academy for Spiritual Formation, a program of The Upper Room. I spent years and years in therapy trying to heal from my trauma. And while I made great progress, I always hit a wall at the same place every time. The years of fear and night terrors made it clear I still had work to do, but every time I tried to access particular feelings or to process specific events, I'd strike out. All that changed when I went to The Academy. There I encountered God in a way I never had before. It was profound, life-altering, game-changing, surprising, and gorgeous. For the first time I could tell my story of pain and despair to God. I ranted and raved, grieved and questioned. I threw the most unholy of adult tantrums, one that was forty-plus years in the making. And like Job, I sat in the midst of my desolation and waited for God's response. And God *did* respond in the most gentle and glorious way. Over and over, God responded, and slowly I began to heal. I realized that the missing piece for me in all those years of therapy was the spiritual piece; I had dealt with the physical and emotional pain, but I hadn't addressed the spiritual pain. The Academy helped me do that.

Obviously I am not shy about promoting The Academy for Spiritual Formation. Like anyone who's been on the mountaintop, I've got the zealous desire to take everyone back up with me. It worked wonders for me and, from my perspective, it did the same for most of the fifty other folks who were part of my Academy #34 class. Now in its thirty-third year, The Academy model has proven over and over to be effective and life-changing through its focus on silence and solitude, prayer and worship, reading and lectures, and group interaction. It works. I've provided information about The Academy at the back of this book on the off chance that you'll check it out and sign up.

But here's the deal: You don't have to go to The Academy to heal from trauma. You may not have the time, money, or interest. And it's not the only game in town; many other programs can effectively facilitate spiritual healing.

The Academy worked for me because it gave me the space and the time (more than just a weekend) and the support to be still. In that repetitive, sustained stillness I encountered God, mustered up the courage to speak my truth, listened for a response, heard it, and began to heal. It's the being still

that is the real game-changer. In our crazy-busy, hyperconnected, noisy lives
we rarely take time to be still. That's particularly true for us trauma survivors
who stay busy and plugged in exactly so we *don't* have to be still. We know
that in the stillness we will hear things we'd rather not hear: fear, anger, grief,
and other feelings associated with the trauma. But The Academy taught me
that God's voice of deep, healing love proves stronger than our pain; and
when we bring that pain to the Light, God transforms it into something holy.
Then we can move on to become who God created us to be.

In this book I attempt to take some core elements of The Academy—
being still with God through scripture reading, group sharing, prayer, and
reflection—and weave them together with my story in a way that fosters
healing. The tool that will help us do that is prayer beads.

I am a Protestant girl (raised Presbyterian, now United Methodist) who
was always drawn to the Catholic rosary and other tools that people around
the world used to connect with God. I collected beads but never prayed
with them, mostly because I wasn't praying much in the first place. In 2009
I experienced a very quirky calling from which I learned about Protestant
(Anglican) prayer beads. I began to make, teach, and write about them, and
have built what is now a full-time ministry on prayer and prayer beads. Along
with The Academy, the prayer beads taught me how to be still and listen to
God, and I've seen them serve a similar function for hundreds of others as well.
Over the past seven years I've witnessed or received profound testimonies
from folks about the prayer beads. They tell stories of encountering God in
new ways, deepening their prayer lives, returning to church after long periods
of exile, and experiencing God's deep love.

There were also stories—lots of them—about how the prayer beads
helped folks feel God's presence with them during times of trial. The more I
heard them, the more I realized it wasn't just me: Prayer beads could benefit
people who hold spiritual pain. To test this theory, I began leading a prayer
bead workshop for soldiers with PTSD. I admit I felt hesitant: I wasn't at all
sure how they would receive me and my box of beads, but I showed up. I
shared my story of trauma and healing, talked about the benefits of using
prayer beads, invited them to make their own sets, then held my breath. To
my delight and amazement, they accepted my invitation, creating sets that
reflected their traumas and varied faiths, their individual histories, their fears
and hopes. Many have since shared how the beads help calm their anxiety,
provide way to process their experience, and remind them they are not alone.

That's why I'm convinced that prayer beads can help those of us trying to heal from spiritual wounds. Prayer beads will help us:

- *speak our truth.* Healing from trauma begins with telling our stories. In sharing our experiences, survivors can process the trauma, receive support, and begin to understand that the trauma does not define us. Trouble is, we are often discouraged to tell our stories. In many cases, we muffle our own voices, fearful that in telling our stories we will relive the pain. But more often, the world tells us to keep quiet so as not to offend or worry those around us. This causes a host of problems, not the least of which is that we begin to believe we should never tell our story—not even to God. Prayer beads can offer a path to begin to tell our stories. They can carve out a "safe space" from which to share our most intimate thoughts. In a sense, rather than looking God in the eyes, which can feel intimidating, we can focus on the beads as we talk. And they can offer a concrete, sacramental reminder of God's presence with us, helping us to know that God is listening to what we have to say.

- *heal our spirit.* As we begin to tell our stories we can recognize the ways in which the trauma affected our relationship with God. We can put names on feelings: grief, shame, anger, fear. We can accuse God of abandoning or punishing us. We can rant, rave, cry, and be hysterical. We can be honest with God, more so than we've been with anyone on earth. Such truth-telling allows us to engage in honest dialogue with God, perhaps for the first time. In that dialogue we will begin to hear God's truth, God's words of healing and deep love. Prayer beads can provide structure for this dialogue and encourage us to be still and to listen for God's voice. They can help us refocus when our minds start to wander. Using tactile objects such as prayer beads can get us out of our heads so we connect our thoughts and feelings with our bodies—something that survivors often find difficult to do. Holding the beads grounds us. We are able to notice our breath, identify any tension in our bodies, and recognize our physical responses to thoughts and feelings. In other words, the beads can reveal the body's wisdom, inviting us to tap into it and experience calm. And the beads can show us that God is experiencing our feelings with us, given that God is as close to us as the beads between our fingers.

- *experience God's peace.* Having entered into true dialogue with God, trauma survivors can begin to develop a relationship of trust. We begin to speak of gratitude. We understand we can rely on God in all circumstances and that God will never abandon us. We start to accept this is true because of God's deep love. Here we practice living in wholeness, using our prayer beads to praise God from whom all blessings flow.

These three areas form the structure of this study. And each chapter will include the following elements: a scripture passage that supports the chapter theme; truth-telling, where I discuss the chapter theme from my perspective; reflection questions to give you a chance to ponder the chapter theme and content from your own perspective; a prayer bead experience (a guided prayer to use with your prayer beads) that connects with the reflection questions, offering a chance to share your particular perspective with God; and a listening focus (a single line to be repeated with your prayer beads) designed to help you relax, be still, and listen to God's healing voice in your life. You may even find yourself repeating the listening focus throughout the day as you drive to work or do the dishes, enabling the words to seep into your being as you process their meaning. The last element (What Do You Notice?) offers a chance to check in with yourself: space to identify thoughts and feelings that may have come up from the chapter material, time to consider whom you can share this with, and an opportunity to use the prayer beads to connect with your body and take a deep breath before you move forward. Feel free to come back to this exercise as many times as necessary. I also encourage you to have a journal handy for this exercise as well as for the other chapter elements.

You may not buy in to the whole prayer bead thing. That's okay. It's not a requirement for spiritual healing. But I hope you'll stick with me and keep reading. You may find other aspects that are useful in your healing journey. At the very least, you have a community of folks who are on a similar path and cheering you on. That's worth something. A whole lot in fact.

A FEW CAVEATS

Writing a book on spiritual healing requires care. There's a lot at stake. As such, here are a few items, in the spirit of truth-telling, to consider before we begin:

- I am not a therapist, counselor, spiritual director, or other practitioner. I do not have formal training in these fields. I do have practical experience: from 1988 to 2002 I worked full-time in the areas of domestic violence, sexual assault, and criminal justice (where there are many survivors). I directed rape crisis centers, responded to middle-of-the-night pages to sit with rape victims in the emergency room, developed training programs, and promoted public policy changes to address these issues. Some of those experiences underlie the words in this book, but mostly I speak as a trauma survivor.

- Given my lack of formal training in psychology and counseling, I made sure that people with those backgrounds had some involvement in this book. A number of therapists, spiritual directors, pastors, and other professionals reviewed the material and provided feedback. This book carries their input and voices as well.

- I *strongly* encourage you to undertake this study with others. Don't go this alone. Make sure you have a therapist, spiritual director, pastor, or support group with you. In addition, identify particular friends and loved ones to serve as your support system. Reading about trauma may stir up painful memories, feelings, and questions. And speaking your truth before God is no small thing. You will need a community to support you, encourage you, catch you if you fall, and celebrate when you hit the high notes and hear the angels sing.

- Traumas don't all look the same. Although I am a survivor of childhood sexual assault, I designed this book to address a broader range of trauma: abuse (physical, psychological, sexual), accident or natural disaster, bullying, combat or military trauma, cultic abuse, sudden death of a loved one, victim or witness to violent crime (unfortunately, the list could go on). Although people experience traumatic events differently (even people who survive the same event will have varying reactions), some spiritual issues are common to most: feelings of abandonment, grief, anger, shame, mistrust, difficulty with forgiveness, and a desire for peace and wholeness. Focus on the areas that speak to you, and disregard the rest.

- Because traumas don't look the same and because mine is not the only story of healing, I had intended to include stories from other survivors in this book. Unfortunately, I had the problem of too much good content and not enough space. But we can use this to our advantage by placing the bonus content online where we can develop a community of healing. I hope you'll check out my new website: http://beadsofhealing.com, where I will post bonus stories and content related to this book. Share your story, post comments, gather around the table. Together, we will create a more complete vision of God's grace.

- I do not intend this study to be linear. That's why there are no chapter numbers. People heal at different rates and may deal with issues in a different order than that laid out in the book (particularly the section on Healing Your Spirit). Feel free to take your time; pace yourself; even skip around as necessary, reading chapters that address where you are at a given point in time. No one's keeping score. You won't get bonus points for reading every page in order. This is *your* healing journey; own it and create something fabulous.

- Although this book follows my two previous books on Protestant prayer beads, I will not assume you are familiar with their content. If you have never used prayer beads before, I invite you to review A Guide to Using Prayer Beads (page 135) before you begin the first chapter. This will help you when you reach the prayer bead experience at the end of each chapter.

- I offer my story to you in the high hopes that it will serve as a witness to God's healing grace and offer ways for you to experience such grace as well. But do not compare your journey to mine or anyone else's. Even if we had all experienced the same trauma, the way we reacted to it, understood it, survived it, and healed from it would differ for each of us. And we have not had the same experience. See your journey for what it is: *your* journey, one that is unique to you. Learn what you can from me or others; but in the end, own your own healing process and understand you will heal in your own time and in your own way. God is limitless, and so are the ways in which God offers us grace.

Above all else, know this: This is a story of love—*deep* love—one that begins and ends with God. It's also a story of how that divine love sustained me through a period of total darkness and terror; patiently bore my anger, mistrust, and grief; and finally led me to a place of healing, tender gratitude, peace, and wholeness.

Here's how it goes.

PROLOGUE

Hide-and-Seek

It was a warm summer day. I know that because I was wearing my favorite Holly Hobbie halter top and matching blue shorts. And I know that because my friends and I had spent the whole afternoon playing hide-and-seek. I loved that game. I was very good at finding those hiding places that no one else could find—those super-duper, totally awesome hiding places.

At some point, my friends went inside. I don't remember why; but I remember knowing they were going to come out pretty soon, so I waited. I sat on the sidewalk, then lay back in the sun to look up at the clouds.

And that's when he approached me.

He was a young guy, maybe early twenties. He had blond hair and was standing with a bicycle. He flashed a wide smile and said, "Hi."

"Hi," I said.

"Looks like you're enjoying the sun," he noted.

"Yep."

"Hey, I've got to gather some newspapers for a friend of mine and there's a lot of them. Would you be willing to help me?" he asked.

Of course, I would. I loved helping people. I was always offering to help my mom—a working single mother—with my one-year-old brother. I liked feeling responsible and helpful at the same time. Even though I was seven, it made me feel older.

"Sure," I replied.

And that's how, on a warm summer day, at the age of seven, I walked away with a complete stranger.

I'll spare you the details. Suffice it to say, we didn't pick up any newspapers.

The damage had been done. But what made it worse was that the young, blond-haired guy with the bicycle threatened me. He said that if I told anyone what he had done, he would come back and kill me and my family. I believed him. I had no reason not to.

And so I walked home to find my friends waiting for me. They were ready to play again and had been wondering where I was. I didn't tell them. Instead, I sat with my head in my hands and just stared.

"What's the matter with you?" they asked, confused by this sudden change in their friend. I remember one of them saying, "She must not feel well."

I didn't respond.

And when my mom called me in for supper, I didn't say anything to her either. I stayed completely silent. I found a hiding place—a super-duper, totally awesome hiding place deep within me—a place no one would be able to find. And I buried that horrible secret.

SPEAKING YOUR TRUTH

Within the echo of the Voice

that spoke us into being

is the sound of our own true voice.

—Robert Benson

The Echo Within: Finding Your True Calling

Choosing to Be Healed

After this there was a feast of the Jews, and Jesus went up to Jerusalem. Now there is in Jerusalem by the Sheep Gate a pool, in Aramaic called Bethesda, which has five roofed colonnades. In these lay a multitude of invalids—blind, lame, and paralyzed. One man was there who had been an invalid for thirty-eight years. When Jesus saw him lying there and knew that he had already been there a long time, he said to him, "Do you want to be healed?" The sick man answered him, "Sir, I have no one to put me into the pool when the water is stirred up, and while I am going another steps down before me." Jesus said to him, "Get up, take up your bed, and walk." And at once the man was healed, and he took up his bed and walked.

Now that day was the Sabbath.

—JOHN 5:1-9, ESV

TRUTH-TELLING

Did I want to be healed? If anyone—including and especially Jesus—had asked me whether I wanted to be healed, I think my head would have exploded. I had prayed so desperately and so long for healing and peace that I was beginning to grow hoarse, weary of my own repetitive pleas for mercy.

At forty-four years of age, I had lived the majority of my life in fear. It took many forms: constant, almost obsessive-compulsive monitoring of locked doors and alarm systems; uncontrollable shaking when dealing with people who were unstable and prone to violent outbursts (which proved problematic during my early social work days); and a complete reluctance to advocate for myself when necessary. The most prominent form of fear in my life, however, was the night terrors that plagued me for more than twenty years. One moment I would be sleeping soundly, safely snuggled between my husband and our cat(s); the next I was leaping out of bed, screaming and thrashing violently. These disturbances were always precipitated by visions that shared one of these three themes: a spider, ghost, or monster was descending upon me; I was being buried or locked in complete, suffocating darkness (which made sense given that the molestation took place in a dark storage closet); or—most commonly—I had been offered a choice (always random and insignificant, such as whether to open a red or a blue door), had chosen wrongly, and was therefore facing sudden death. All resulted in sheer terror. All left my husband, our cats, and me feeling bewildered and groggy the following day.

The fear reached fever pitch in 2011, the year my son, Matthew, was turning seven. For years I had anticipated this would be a tough birthday for me. As my son reached the age I was when I was molested, I knew I would be seeing myself in him, seeing what being seven looked like: the vulnerability, the innocence, the delight, the blind trust in the goodness of the world. I sensed I would relive the trauma even as I would fear for his safety. The closer we got to his birth date, the more anxious I became. My prayers for peace became fanatical, anguished.

Did I want to be healed? Seriously?

I imagine the man beside the Bethesda pool feels the same way when Jesus asks the question. As if he hasn't prayed for healing every day for thirty-eight years. As if he hasn't wished that very thing every hour he lies beside the pool, waiting for the water to stir. As if he hasn't yelled out in frustration, even anger, each time another person beats him to the water.

Jesus knows this, of course. He knows the man's story, his pain, his need for healing. Jesus can easily walk over to the man, kneel beside him, speak some healing words, help the man to his feet, and go on about his day. But he doesn't. Instead, he insists on asking the question, which tells us two things.

First, Jesus will not impose himself on the man and assume he desires healing—with good reason. Jesus understands the man needs to play an active role in his own healing. Think about it. The man has been paralyzed for thirty-eight years. All that time he's depended on others to carry him places, take care of him, even help him into the pool. We can imagine how this would play on his self-esteem, how over time his identity would change to incorporate a sense of dependence and passiveness. Had Jesus just walked up and healed him, the man would have remained in a passive position. But through his question, Jesus invites the man to become an active participant in his own healing journey. For his sake, the man needs to say, "Yes, I want to be healed" before any real healing will take place.

And that is critical. Because the other reason Jesus asks the question is this: Healing is hard. It takes work. Being healed from paralysis represents only the first step in the man's journey. Following that, he will have to learn a whole new way of living. Life will no longer be as he has known it; it will be completely different, and he will have to learn to adjust.

I imagine the man understands this at some level. You can hear it in his response to Jesus' question. Does he sound defensive? Whiney? Hopeless? Doubtful? Indignant? It could be any or all or even none of those things. What strikes me though, is that when Jesus asks him if he wants to be healed, the man does not immediately answer, "Yes! Please!" Instead, he gives a long list of reasons why he can't get well.

We have all done this at one time or another. We have explained, complained, and made excuses for why we continue to deal with troubling issues. Whether the trauma was in the recent or distant past, we have all had times when we throw pity parties and sulk at the feet of Jesus. All the excuses are part of the process, which is why we read no judgment here. Jesus listens patiently, lovingly, as the man tells his story of woe, never once chiding or condemning him.

Still Jesus challenges the man. Through this simple question Jesus makes it clear that healing carries responsibility. In addition to learning an entirely new way of living, the man will have to learn a whole new way of interacting with God and others. He'll have to step out of his comfort zone and take risks in order to progress. He'll be asked to help others who need healing, to share his story and struggle and prayers so that others may find healing in Jesus. Things are going to change. Jesus wants the man to be ready.

I confess I wasn't ready when I first heard Jesus' question. The question came about six months after Matthew's seventh birthday and not in the way I expected. In the place of Jesus was a man named Johnny Sears, Director of The Upper Room's Academy for Spiritual Formation. And instead of asking, "Do you want to be healed?" he asked, "Do you want to come to The Academy?"

I had read about The Academy in a brochure. I read with some interest about the program, which uses silence and solitude, worship, lectures, and group reflection to promote spiritual formation. I was interested enough to take the brochure home and do further research online, where I learned there were two types of Academies: Five-Day and Two-Year. Never being one to dip my toe into the water when I can dive in head first, I decided I would go the Two-Year route when and if I had the time and money. At that time, I had neither. And so, much like the man beside the Bethesda pool, I offered my excuses for not going. Johnny remained undaunted.

"We've got a scholarship program and can help you seek grants."

I promised to think about it. Johnny promised to follow up.

And so he did. Every time I saw the man, he asked, "Have you started your application yet?"

I had not, but that didn't mean I wasn't considering it. At the time, my prayer bead ministry was new but already showing signs of success. The potential for its growth seemed obvious, and clearly God was calling me to continue. I figured The Academy would provide the perfect opportunity for me to reflect on this calling and gain a deeper understanding of how I could use it to glorify God.

Finally, I applied and was accepted. My home conference of The United Methodist Church provided a grant, which The Upper Room matched. Some family and friends kicked in funds as well. I cleared my calendar—a total of eight weeks over the next two years. In August of 2012 I headed for Camp Sumatanga in Gallant, Alabama, ready to explore my calling to this prayer bead ministry.

Turns out, that's not why God led me to The Academy. What I didn't know then was that The Academy would be my place of healing from trauma. It would be the answer to my relentless prayers for peace. It would be Jesus looking at me and declaring, "Get up, take up your bed, and walk!" It would be the origin of my path to learning a new way of being.

Do you want to be healed?

Are you ready to play an active role in your healing journey? Are you ready to say yes to Jesus, knowing that your answer will be just the beginning? Knowing it will lead to hard work, tough times, up-and-down days, difficult decisions, periods when you simply don't want to get out of bed? But knowing too that it will lead to moments of great insight and growth, incredible joy, and a life full of God's grace?

It's okay if you aren't ready. Really. Not everyone will be. You may need time to ponder all this. If that's the case, do it. This is your healing journey, not anyone else's—so you are the expert. Give yourself time to pray and listen to your heart. Trust yourself, knowing that you can say yes in your own time. There is no need to rush. From all I've seen, Jesus is a pretty patient guy who loves you deeply and will love you into your moment of truth, whenever that is.

Trust him. Trust yourself. And be healed.

REFLECTION QUESTIONS

1. Where do you see yourself in this story of the man by the Bethesda pool?
2. Why do you believe Jesus asked the man if he wanted to be healed?
3. When have you heard this question in your life? What did it sound like? What was your response?
4. Do you want to be healed? Why or why not?
5. Do you feel like a passive or active participant in your healing journey? If you feel passive, what will help you feel active?
6. What does healing look like for you? What will you need for your healing journey?
7. The man by the pool was not alone in his healing; Jesus was with him. Who will accompany you on your journey? What will your support system look like?

PRAYER BEAD EXPERIENCE

Cross: God of light,

Invitatory bead: help me to speak my truth

Resurrection bead: by the power of your Son, Jesus Christ.

1st cruciform bead: I hear Jesus asking me, "Do you want to be healed?"

Week beads, set 1: Use each bead to listen to Jesus' question.

2nd cruciform bead: I wonder if I am truly ready to be healed.

Week beads, set 2: Use each bead to lift up any fears, concerns, or questions you may have about your readiness to be healed.

3rd cruciform bead: I don't know what to expect on my healing journey.

Week beads, set 3: Use each bead to envision what your healing journey might look like, being as specific as possible. What will you feel, what will happen, who will be involved, what will you need, where can you go for comfort, and what activities will nurture you along the way?

4th cruciform bead: I ask for your help and guidance along the way.

Week beads, set 4: Use each bead to pray for a sense of God's presence, comfort, and guidance along your healing journey.

Resurrection bead: In the name of your Son, Jesus Christ,

Invitatory bead: who has the power to heal me.

Cross: Amen.

Listening Focus

Choose from the following options for a Listening Focus, depending upon how you answered Reflection Question #4.

> Option one: Do I want to be healed?
> Option two: Yes, I want to be healed!
> Option three: I don't feel ready to be healed. Help me.

What Do You Notice?

What insights, feelings, memories, or other wisdom arose as you read the chapter material or completed the prayer bead experience? Whom can you share this with?

Take a minute to use your prayer beads to connect with your body. Sit quietly and breathe deeply with each bead. As you do, stay present in the moment, releasing any concerns, anxiety, or distractions. Embrace this place of stillness with God before you continue in your journey.

BEING STILL

Now Ahab told Jezebel everything Elijah had done and how he had killed all the prophets with the sword. So Jezebel sent a messenger to Elijah to say, "May the gods deal with me, be it ever so severely, if by this time tomorrow I do not make your life like that of one of them."

Elijah was afraid and ran for his life. When he came to Beersheba in Judah, he left his servant there, while he himself went a day's journey into the wilderness. He came to a broom bush, sat down under it and prayed that he might die. "I have had enough, LORD," he said. "Take my life; I am no better than my ancestors." Then he lay down under the bush and fell asleep.

All at once an angel touched him and said, "Get up and eat." He looked around, and there by his head was some bread baked over hot coals, and a jar of water. He ate and drank and then lay down again.

The angel of the LORD came back a second time and touched him and said, "Get up and eat, for the journey is too much for you." So he got up and ate and drank. Strengthened by that food, he traveled forty days and forty nights until he reached Horeb, the mountain of God. There he went into a cave and spent the night.

And the word of the LORD came to him: "What are you doing here, Elijah?"

He replied, "I have been very zealous for the LORD God Almighty. The Israelites have rejected your covenant, torn down your altars, and put your prophets to death with the sword. I am the only one left, and now they are trying to kill me too."

The LORD said, "Go out and stand on the mountain in the presence of the LORD, for the LORD is about to pass by."

Then a great and powerful wind tore the mountains apart and shattered the rocks before the LORD, but the LORD was not in the wind. After the wind there was an earthquake, but the LORD was not in the earthquake. After the earthquake came a fire, but the LORD was not in the fire. And after the fire came a gentle whisper.

—1 KINGS 19:1-12, NIV

TRUTH-TELLING

NOTE: In the year I spent planning this book and drafting outlines, the following chapter was never part of the mix. But the day after I finished the previous chapter, I was walking my dog and suddenly thought, *There will be a chapter on being still.* And in the same moment I was astonished I'd never thought of this before. You'll understand why. So here it is: the chapter that insisted on being included.

The Academy model is all about rhythm, particularly for the Two-Year program. For two years you pack up your bags every three months to go away for five days. Once you've arrived, you settle into the rhythm of the session: morning prayer, breakfast, lecture, silent reflection, group sharing, lunch, free time, lecture, silent reflection, group sharing, Eucharist, dinner, covenant group meetings, night prayer, and silence (which is broken only by morning prayer the next day). It is the same every day, every session, every year, and has been so for more than thirty-three years.

This rhythm accounts for The Academy's effectiveness; at its heart resides an emphasis on being still. The Academy calls us out of our busy lives to sit with God, to listen and pay attention.

The concept of being still really appealed to me. I entered The Academy a Type-A overachiever—a whirling dervish of motion, ideas, lists, and responsibilities. I rarely sat still and seldom took time to listen. Before getting in the car, I submitted the manuscript for my first book, *A Bead and a Prayer,* to Upper Room Books. I arrived at Camp Sumatanga two hours early, feeling accomplished and ready to use the next two years to explore my calling and see what else I could achieve. I had this being-still thing in the bag.

The burst in my Type-A bubble was swift, breathtaking. During Eucharist on our first full day, I walked up to receive the elements. As I did, I heard a soft voice within me say, "I feel safe here."

Wow, I thought, *how wonderful to know I feel safe here. This is going to be great.* And I moved on.

Two days later, during a time of silent reflection, I heard the same soft voice. This time it stopped me in my tracks.

"That was me who said 'I feel safe here.'"

Instinctively, I knew who that soft, little voice belonged to: my seven-year-old self. After thirty-eight years, little Kristie was emerging for the first time from her super-duper, totally awesome, hiding place. She recognized that this setting offered something she had never had before: a safe place; a chance for her to be still long enough to hear her sweet, small voice; an opportunity for her to sit with the God of healing and share her story of deepest pain.

Suddenly, I developed an awareness of a separate part of myself, a part that had been hiding most of my life and was now asking to be heard. I found the experience a little unnerving—startling but also exhilarating. I understood immediately that I had figured this Academy adventure all wrong: It was not going to be primarily about my work with prayer beads. First and foremost, it was going to be about healing from the trauma I had suffered and survived all those years ago. It was going to be profound, life-changing, and beautiful— everything I had prayed for and desired most. And it scared me to death. Be careful what you wish for they say. *Be careful what you pray for,* I thought. Was I ready for an answer to my lifelong prayer?

Not quite, because even as I went home to tell everyone about this profound experience and share my excitement about The Academy, I unconsciously began to fight stillness. As much as I wanted to be still and be healed, the idea of its actually happening scared me. I couldn't imagine what else I would hear or feel. I didn't know how this healing experience would play out or how it would change my life. I was weary of feeling fearful. But fear, like an old, worn-out cardigan that needed to be discarded, was familiar. I knew what to expect of it. By the time November rolled around, I headed to my second Academy session fully armed. I arrived late and stressed, carrying my computer, a stack of work, and a list of excuses for why I couldn't be still.

❖

Being still is hard, particularly in this day and age. Noise surrounds us; messages and alerts bombard us; supervisors ask us to work harder and produce more. When we do rest or take a break, we feel guilty, offering excuses and promising to work harder to make up for lost time. Add trauma to the mix, and being still becomes almost impossible. Movement and busyness keep the feelings at bay. Noise drowns out the memories and numbs the pain. The idea of creating space for the pain is terrifying, as we see in our scripture passage.

Elijah is traumatized. Queen Jezebel wants to kill him, so Elijah runs for his life, literally. He runs and runs until he can't run anymore. In the process, he ditches his assistant, the person whose job it is to support him. Finally, he reaches a desolate and remote place that provides only one lonely bush to sit under. There, he asks God to kill him. I don't judge him for that. While I never reached the point where I considered suicide, I have had moments where I said to God, "I can't do this anymore. I'm done." Elijah had clearly reached his breaking point.

Of course, the Lord does not agree to Elijah's suicide plan. Recognizing Elijah's frail emotional state, God instead sends an angel to minister to him. I imagine that Elijah's extreme exhaustion and experience of trauma prevented his recognizing this angel as sent from God. He probably doesn't even acknowledge this act of kindness. Still, the angel's ministry is so effective that Elijah journeys for forty straight days through the desert until he reaches the place to which God is calling him: Mount Horeb. There, God asks Elijah, "What are you doing here?"

It seems like we've been here before. Like Jesus' question to the paralyzed man in the previous chapter, God's question to Elijah seems obvious. Again, I can imagine Elijah's response: "Really? Do you really have to ask what I'm doing here? Do I have to spell it out for you?" The answer, of course, is yes. God knows Elijah needs to pour out his heart to God, to name and recognize his feelings, concerns, and anxieties. And it is crucial that Elijah do that with God. Elijah needs to learn he can be still and honest and even angry with God. God offers Elijah an opportunity to rant and rave—a necessary part of the healing process—and Elijah takes God up on it. And when he finishes, God invites him to come out of his cave, to emerge from the place that holds his pain, and to be with God.

And here is just one way to interpret the next part of the passage: I think we see what Elijah believes will happen when he is still and vulnerable; what he imagines will take place when he comes before the Lord with his trauma, having exposed all his pain. He figures scary things will happen. He anticipates that it will be awful and terrifying, that the world will end in a storm of catastrophic wind, earthquakes, and/or fire. He worries about being consumed by his pain. He's expecting that no good can come from this.

But Elijah is safe. Because God is not in the catastrophic wind, the earthquakes, *or* the fire. Instead, Elijah encounters God in the peace and quiet. In the stillness. In the gentle whisper of the One who has been with him and ministering to him all this time. When he uncovers the depth of his pain, Elijah encounters the God who can transform that raging pain into a quiet, gentle peace—a peace that is healing and grace-filled.

I do not judge Elijah for the way he handled his trauma. I get it. For many years I ran with and from the pain of my trauma. I too ditched my assistants, those people God placed in my path to help me. I too missed the times when God tried to minister directly to me. I too ranted and raved when I felt that God was doing nothing about my pain. I too expected scary things to happen if I stayed still too long and listened to God's response. I feel sure that many of you get it as well.

But here's the thing: We can't do this forever. We can't keep up this pace and continue to drop the folks who want to help us and avoid the God who loves us deeply. We just can't. We weren't built to go it alone. More to the point, the Holy One created us to love God, ourselves, and others; we can't do that if we're mired in pain. So we've got to be still. Our very lives depend on it. It's in the stillness that we find our truth.

Being still is scary; it involves surrender and vulnerability. When we're still, we can't control things—and that's hard. It doesn't come naturally, especially when what we're trying to control is our heart's pain. Odd thing is that when we finally surrender, we realize we were never in control in the first place.

I can promise you this: It's gonna be okay. You will survive being still. Not only that, you will find God. One of my favorite scripture verses is Psalm 46:10: "Be still, and know that I am God." When you are still, you will finally come to know God for who God is: a God of peace, healing, and comfort. That's what I found when I finally embraced being still at The Academy. And though it's been two years since I graduated from The Academy, I have continued to practice being still every day. It's an integral part of my life. I have found many ways to be quiet with God on a daily basis. I now crave and even enjoy being still, especially when life isn't going so well. I trust that I can bring my pain and questions to God and know I will come away with clarity (sometimes), peace (most of the time), and a sense of God's presence (all of the time).

The good news is you can start small. Take baby steps as you practice being still. Sit outside and watch the birds for five minutes. Use an app such as calm.com for two minutes. Write one paragraph in your journal. Try praying. Turn the radio off when you're in the car. Grab a coloring book and some crayons. It doesn't matter how, when, or how long; get creative and incorporate options that fit your comfort level. When you discover that you're comfortable being still for small amounts of time, build up from there. Refrain from comparing yourself to anyone else; this is your journey, so own everything about it, including how you choose to be still with God.

Now go and be still, listening for the gentle whisper of God.

REFLECTION QUESTIONS

1. How do you see yourself in this story of Elijah?
2. What do you imagine Elijah was feeling up on Mount Horeb?
3. How would you answer God's question, "What are you doing here?"
4. Who are the people in your life who support or help you? When have you ditched them and tried to go it alone? What happened?
5. Can you look back in your life and see times when God ministered to you, though you may not have recognized it at the time? Describe them.
6. Does being still feel threatening? If so, how and why?
7. Where in your life can you make room for stillness? How and when?

Prayer Bead Experience

Cross: God of light,

Invitatory bead: help me to speak my truth

Resurrection bead: by the power of your Son, Jesus Christ.

1ˢᵗ cruciform bead: I hear you asking me, "What are you doing here?"

Week beads, set 1: Use each bead to listen to God's question for you.

2ⁿᵈ cruciform bead: I have no answers or many answers to that question.

Week beads, set 2: Use each bead to consider how you would answer God's question.

3ʳᵈ cruciform bead: I hear you calling me to be still so that I may hear your gentle whisper.

Week beads, set 3: Use each bead to listen to God's call to you to be still. Can you begin to hear God's gentle whisper? How does that make you feel? What do you imagine will happen when you are still?

4ᵗʰ cruciform bead: I need your help to be still so that I may be healed.

Week beads, set 4: Use each bead to pray for God's help to be still and for a sense of God's presence, comfort, and guidance along your healing journey.

Resurrection bead: In the name of your Son, Jesus Christ,

Invitatory bead: who has the power to heal me.

Cross: Amen.

Listening Focus

"Be still, and know that I am God!" (Ps. 46:10, NRSV).

What Do You Notice?

What insights, feelings, memories, or other wisdom arose as you read the chapter material or completed the prayer bead experience? Whom can you share this with?

Take a minute to use your prayer beads to connect with your body. Sit quietly and breathe deeply with each bead. As you do, stay present in the moment, releasing any concerns, anxiety, or distractions. Embrace this place of stillness with God before you continue in your journey.

SPEAKING YOUR TRUTH

A swarm of people were following Jesus, crowding in on him. A woman was there who had been bleeding for twelve years. She had suffered a lot under the care of many doctors, and had spent everything she had without getting any better. In fact, she had gotten worse. Because she had heard about Jesus, she came up behind him in the crowd and touched his clothes. She was thinking, If I can just touch his clothes, I'll be healed. Her bleeding stopped immediately, and she sensed in her body that her illness had been healed.

At that very moment, Jesus recognized that power had gone out from him. He turned around in the crowd and said, "Who touched my clothes?"

His disciples said to him, "Don't you see the crowd pressing against you? Yet you ask, 'Who touched me?'" But Jesus looked around carefully to see who had done it.

The woman, full of fear and trembling, came forward. Knowing what had happened to her, she fell down in front of Jesus and told him the whole truth. He responded, "Daughter, your faith has healed you; go in peace, healed from your disease."

—MARK 5:25-34

TRUTH-TELLING

During the first session of The Academy, Irene, the worship leader, encouraged participants to help lead the three daily worship services. She posted a chart with the list of services for each of the next seven sessions. Opportunities

33

ranged from serving as liturgist or celebrant to preaching or leading the music to designing the altar settings.

"We invite you to step out of your comfort zone," Irene explained. "If you preach regularly, try an altar design. If you always sing, try preaching. If you don't usually speak in front of groups, sign up to be the liturgist."

I do public speaking all the time, but I don't do much preaching. I'm married to a gifted preacher, and one preacher per household seems sufficient. But for whatever reason, the preaching opportunity popped into my head while Irene spoke. I looked over the chart to view my options.

As I've said before, The Academy is about rhythm. In addition to the rhythm of the days themselves, each session has a rhythm. Every day has an assigned theme. The daily theme took us on a journey throughout the week, allowing us to leave the world temporarily to go deeper into our spiritual lives, then prepare us for reentry. For example, session two themes were Creation, Call, Covenant, Exile, Promise, Hope. We start with something "easy" like Creation or Call; but by midweek when everyone has generally settled in and begun to get real with God, we reach a place of Exile. Participants would work through whatever Exile meant for them, then spend the remaining two days moving to a place of Hope, which, if all went well, provided the place from which they would reenter the world.

Glancing over the worship chart, I stopped at the fourth day of session three. The theme for that day was Abandonment. As soon as I read the word, I realized I would preach that day and tell my story of trauma. I signed my name, committing to step out of my comfort zone in more ways than one.

Granted, this would not be my first time to tell the story of what happened when I was seven. I had made other attempts. At age twelve I first broke my silence about the molestation. Hanging out with my best friend, Barbara, one day, I said, "When I was seven, I was raped." *Raped* was the only word I had to describe what happened to me; I had heard it explained one time and immediately connected it to my experience. It would be years before I learned there was an entire continuum of sexual violence.

"Really? What happened?" Barbara asked.

I told her the story as best I could.

"That's not rape," she countered. Barbara prided herself on knowing a lot of things and was often blunt about it.

Technically speaking, Barbara was right. And the larger issue was that neither of us had the emotional intelligence to handle such truth-telling. But

I didn't understand that. All I could process was the harsh reaction of the first person I tried to tell. I heard judgment and disbelief, and I quickly tucked that secret back into its hiding place.

In my early twenties I tried again. By then I was volunteering for the Austin Rape Crisis Center (now Safe Place), serving as a peer supporter and accompanying victims to the hospital for forensic exams, often in the middle of the night. Through the friendships I developed with many of the Center's staff and the other volunteers, I had several opportunities to practice telling my story. Each telling resulted in validation and empathy. This built my confidence enough to share my story with the man who would become my husband. Max received it with the tender love and grace I would hope for in the man I would marry. Later, at age thirty-one, I finally told my mom what had happened all those years ago. She was shocked, grieved, loving, gentle. From her response I realized she would have been the safe refuge I needed had I been able to convey the trauma at the time it occurred.

I received a similar response from the members of my covenant group. During the first session of The Academy participants are assigned to a group of six to eight people who journey with them for the entire two-year period. For ninety minutes each night, we processed the day, reflected on presentations and readings, spoke our truth, raised questions of faith, and learned to be vulnerable in community. The environment was nonjudgmental and confidential, making it feel completely safe. I felt like I had won the covenant-group lottery when I met my group. Amy, Horace, Janet, Lana, Nell, Steve, and I bonded quickly, creating a space of safety, laughter, insight, and deep love. While I anticipated sharing my story of trauma with them at some point in our time together, having heard my seven-year-old voice prompted me to speak up in session one. From then on, my covenant group became an integral part of my healing, offering signs of God's love at all the right times.

These experiences of sharing my story and being validated gave rise to a growing confidence within me. Perhaps I could share it with the entire Academy and live to tell. Recounting my childhood trauma would constitute my "coming out" story, my way of claiming publicly an experience that had hitherto been my life's deepest secret. In speaking my truth, I would proclaim that this trauma had occurred and, while it did not define me, it was one piece of who I am and a significant part of my travels with God. I hoped that in my sharing of it, I could point to the hope and healing available for the taking if we could simply be still.

For months I thought and fretted about the sermon. I worried about what I would say, but I also worried about the response. I knew from experience that my story of trauma could be hard for everyone else to hear. Indeed, that's part of what had kept me silent for so long. One big problem with speaking your truth is that often others don't want to hear your story. It's not personal; but generally speaking, people have a low tolerance for pain and don't know what to do with other people's trauma. Such stories remind them that evil exists in the world, and they would much rather not face that truth. The stories may also remind them of the pain in their own lives, which they've probably tried to forget. And in many instances, those who hear have no idea what to say in response, so they don't say anything. Or they say inappropriate things. They definitely don't ask for more information, offer a listening ear, or admit they don't know what to say and ask for guidance.

The other aspect that kept me silent was shame. I blamed myself for the molestation; it had occurred because I made the wrong decision and had agreed to walk away with that young blond guy with the bike. Of course, it wasn't my fault, but I didn't know that for the longest time.

Lastly, I had held on to my story of trauma for so long that I had come to believe it defined me. I was a Sexual Assault Survivor. Period. I was victimized, damaged, silenced. Sure, I was also a wife, mom, daughter, sister, friend, coworker. But I was a *traumatized* wife, mom, daughter. I would never *not* be a trauma survivor. I saw no opportunity for change. End of story.

I imagine thoughts like these are going through the woman's mind when she approaches Jesus. Indeed, the Bible tells us she tries to be surreptitious in her effort to be healed. She doesn't want any attention and hopes no one will notice as she reaches for the fringed hem of Jesus' robe. After spending twelve years in exile, she knows her shame marks her as one unwelcome. She wants to be healed and then go about her business. But that's not what happens.

Jesus senses this moment of healing and in what we have now established as true God fashion asks an obvious question: "Who touched my clothes?" The poor disciples are at a loss for words. But Jesus has a reason for the question. It requires the woman to identify herself rather than sneaking away—a move born of shame. He encourages her to speak up, to overcome her sense of shame, and to speak her truth for the first time. He wants her to understand that she need not accept the socially imposed shame; she is worthy of being heard and healed; worthy of God's time, attention, and deep love.

Brené Brown, one of my favorite contemporary writers and speakers, has clearly touched a nerve in our world in her groundbreaking work on shame and vulnerability. Her 2010 Tedx Houston talk "The Power of Vulnerability" is one of the top five most viewed Ted Talks in the world. Her books have consistently been #1 *New York Times* best sellers. In her Ted Talk, Dr. Brown describes six years of research on *connection*. She believes that connection, the need to belong, gives our lives meaning and purpose. From a spiritual perspective, I think she's right on the money. Our connection with God, ourselves, and others gives our life meaning. God created us for connection, and Jesus tells us the greatest commandment is to love God with our whole being and to love our neighbors as (and) ourselves.

In her research, Dr. Brown found that the opposite of connection— disconnection and exclusion—results from shame. How can people connect with God or others if they don't feel worthy; if they don't feel good enough, talented enough, thin enough, and so on? These feelings of unworthiness are particularly true for trauma survivors who often carry dark secrets, guilt, and other burdens that get in the way of connection. Dr. Brown goes on to explain that vulnerability is the key to feeling worthy of connection and love.

Anyone else excited about that news? I'm guessing not. For many of us, vulnerability hasn't always worked in our favor. Vulnerability often represents the time(s) when we were hurt in some way and from then on we chose to be anything but vulnerable in order to survive. I know I've spent much of my life hiding my secret, burying my feelings, trying to look brave and happy, and doing what was necessary to fit in and be loved. In other words, trying to be anything but vulnerable.

And guess what? My lack of vulnerability created disconnection. I never actually felt connected to God, myself, or anyone else. I was always hiding something, always trying to be something I wasn't. When I reached the point in my life where I wearied of living this way, I decided I was ready to speak my truth.

Dr. Brown's talk points out that people who had previously been disconnected found connection when they practiced "excruciating vulnerability." They spoke their truth, which took great courage. Dr. Brown reminds us that the word *courage* comes from the Latin *cor*, which means "heart." The original definition was "telling the story of who you are with your whole heart."

Aha.

Remember in the introduction I shared the definition of trauma that derives from the Greek word meaning "to pierce"? If trauma pierces our hearts, we repair them by speaking our truth: telling the story of who we are with our whole heart. Speaking honestly about who we are is the way to heal our heart. And we are multifaceted. We are—first and foremost, beginning, middle, and end—who God created and calls us to be. We are also everything that has happened along the way: the ups and downs, the highs and lows, the trauma, the pain, the questions, the hope, the joy. By telling our stories, we reject the notion that we should feel shame for any or all of our journey. We reject the need to keep secrets and suffer in silence. We deny the power of shame, which thrives in silence and secrecy. We proclaim our worthiness of God's love and healing. That is what it means to tell the story of who we are with our whole heart. That is courage.

So with his question, Jesus calls the woman into the light. Perhaps she hesitates for a moment, wondering if coming forward is worth the risk. But she has tried everything else; she's spent years and all her money going to various doctors. Rather than getting better, she's only gotten worse. By the time she reaches Jesus, she has nothing left to lose. So she courageously responds, speaking her truth, telling her whole story. Keep in mind, she does this "full of fear and trembling." She is scared. By speaking up she bucks the very laws that have kept her in exile for the past twelve years: It was a violation of Jewish law for a woman who was bleeding to be in contact with others, particularly holy men. But she does it anyway. That is the very definition of courage: Doing something that scares you.

Jesus rewards her courage. Rather than scolding, mocking, or dismissing her, he looks at her and calls her, "Daughter." Listen to that. I can almost hear the emotion, the depth of his compassion and love for her. "Daughter." And with that one word, the woman's heart, pierced by the pain of this disease and social isolation, is made whole. With one word Jesus assures her that she is not defined by her condition. She is so much more; he claims her as a daughter in God's beloved family. With one word, the woman's alienation ends. No longer an outcast but a family member—a daughter, worthy of relationship. He has returned her to a life of connection. Her story will have a new ending.

I believe I sensed this possibility when I decided to speak my truth before all my Academy friends. The closer I got to the appointed day, the more I grasped the hope that was growing inside me. I yearned to be whole again. I desired reconnection. And that's exactly what happened.

In an incredible act of love and connection, my covenant group members asked to pray with me prior to the worship service. Gathered with them in a circle, all my remaining fear fell away to be replaced with peace. I began the sermon with the story that appears here in the Prologue. As soon as I said the words, "And that's how, on a warm summer day, at the age of seven, I walked away with a complete stranger," I took a deep, long breath. I had done it. I had told the story of what happened to me when I was seven, and I didn't die. The bicycle guy didn't come to kill my family. Instead, I had been heard. My story would have a new ending.

When time came in worship to pass the peace, members of my Academy community surrounded me with strong embraces and words of love and encouragement. One of my favorite comments came from a member of the leadership team, who said, "That was a moment of true grace." He was right; God's grace was clearly present in the room. Later, people continued to come up to me to thank me for speaking my truth. Many shared their own stories of trauma. In speaking my truth, I had helped create a safe space in which others could speak theirs. I was not alone; together we would find connection. Together, we would hear Jesus call us beloved sons and daughters.

Telling the story of who you are and what happened to you is hard. It can be exhausting. After the last person left the room following worship, I knelt at the altar and began to sob. While relieved and grateful, I was very tired. It can also be excruciating to put words to memories, feelings, nightmares, exclusion, and everything else. And it's not always safe. We have to share our truth at a time and in a way that is conducive to being heard—really heard. We need to consider carefully who, where, when, and how to speak our truth. We need to create a safe space.

But remaining silent can be even more excruciating. Staying silent keeps us in the place of secrecy, shame, guilt, and disconnection. It perpetuates the lie that the trauma defines us and has power over us. It isolates us, causing us to believe that we are forever alone with our story. It prevents us from healing and living fully into what Dr. Brown calls "the birthplace of joy, creativity, belonging." It robs us of the chance to hear Jesus call us by name.

You are God's beloved daughter or son, the person to whom God offers healing. That is your true story. And it's a story the whole world needs to hear.

REFLECTION QUESTIONS

1. Have you shared your story of trauma with others? If so, how did they react?

2. Why do you think it's important to speak your truth before God and others? What difference can this make for you?

3. What does it mean to you that your condition does not define you? How has your condition defined you up to now? What would it mean to let that go?

4. According to the scripture, the woman has spent years of time and lots of money going to various doctors for healing, though she has never gotten better. What other paths to healing have you tried? What was helpful? What was not helpful?

5. What do you hear in Jesus' response to the woman?

6. How do imagine Jesus would respond to you if you spoke your truth? What would he say to you? What would he call you?

7. How can speaking your truth help with your healing? How can it open you up to the healing process?

Prayer Bead Experience

Cross: God of light,

Invitatory bead: help me to speak my truth

Resurrection bead: by the power of your Son, Jesus Christ.

1ˢᵗ cruciform bead: I hear Jesus encouraging me to tell my story.

Week beads, set 1: Use each bead to listen as Jesus invites you to tell your story.

2ⁿᵈ cruciform bead: I have worried that the story of my trauma defines me.

Week beads, set 2: Use each bead to consider how and when you have felt defined by your trauma.

3ʳᵈ cruciform bead: I have been afraid to tell my story.

Week beads, set 3: Use each bead to offer up your fears about speaking your truth.

4ᵗʰ cruciform bead: I need your help to speak my truth and hear your response.

Week beads, set 4: Use each bead to pray for a sense of God's presence, comfort, and guidance along your healing journey. Listen for the words God is speaking to you in response.

Resurrection bead: In the name of your Son, Jesus Christ,

Invitatory bead: who has the power to heal me.

Cross: Amen.

Listening Focus

I am not my condition. I am God's _____. (Take the response you imagined in question 6 above and use it to fill in the blank. For example, you might say, "I am not my condition. I am God's beloved daughter." You may even name your condition specifically; for example, I might pray, "I am not the molestation. I am God's perfect creation.")

What Do You Notice?

What insights, feelings, memories, or other wisdom arose as you read the chapter material or completed the prayer bead experience? Whom can you share this with?

Take a minute to use your prayer beads to connect with your body. Sit quietly and breathe deeply with each bead. As you do, stay present in the moment, releasing any concerns, anxiety, or distractions. Embrace this place of stillness with God before you continue in your journey.

HEALING YOUR SPIRIT

"Jesus?" [Mack] whispered as his voice choked.
"I feel so lost." A hand reached out and
squeezed his and didn't let go.
"I know, Mack. But it's not true.
I am with you, and I'm not lost."

—William Paul Young, *The Shack*

GRIEF

When Mary arrived where Jesus was and saw him, she fell at his feet
and said, "Lord, if you had been here, my brother wouldn't have died."

When Jesus saw her crying and the Jews who had come with her
crying also, he was deeply disturbed and troubled. He asked, "Where
have you laid him?"

They replied, "Lord, come and see."

Jesus began to cry. The Jews said, "See how much he loved him!"

—JOHN 11:32-36

TRUTH-TELLING

Trauma affected my sleep in ways beyond night terrors. I had my own personal
genre of dreams that I dubbed "grief dreams"—dreams characterized by a
bottomless, unfathomable grief. Something would take place in the dream
that would cause me to cry, but I couldn't cry hard enough, loud enough,
or long enough. I would get frustrated and exhaust myself trying to grieve.
Many times I awoke with tears in my eyes and a feeling of desperation and
fatigue. Like the night terrors, these grief dreams companioned me for years.

I understood what these meant. I knew this was my body's way of trying
to express my grief from the trauma, given that I had been incapable of
releasing these tears at the time it happened. The dreams also made it clear
that the grief I was holding on to was deep and wide. *One day*, I thought, *I'm
going to start crying and not be able to stop.*

That day arrived during my second session of The Academy. I woke up
one morning tired and groggy, the result of tossing and turning throughout
the night. There had even been a few night terrors. I dragged myself out of

bed and to the shower, determined to rise above the fatigue that had settled into my bones. The warm water felt good, but as I turned it off and reached for my towel, a muscle in my back seized up, sending spasms of intense pain throughout my body. The pain continued as I hobbled my way through getting dressed and ready for the day.

The rest of the morning was no better. Arriving at morning prayer, I saw that our word for the day was *exile*. *How appropriate*, I thought. I was beginning to feel like I was in exile. My distant, gloomy mood differed greatly from that of the previous day. I was enjoying this second session of The Academy, had benefited from meaningful conversations with some of my friends, and for the first time in over a year, had built up to running thirty minutes straight, putting me closer to my goal of running a 5K. But here I sat, feeling sullen without knowing why. Every hour, I sank deeper into depression.

"Are you going on the hike today?" my friend Amy asked, knowing I had been excited about the chance to climb up the mountain to Creel Chapel.

"I signed up for it, but I think I'm not going . . . "

"How come?"

"I . . . I think I'm really sad," I said and began to cry.

She put her arms around me. "Can I do anything?"

"No. I just need to go walk the labyrinth. Just pray for me."

I turned and walked quickly out of the conference center toward the auditorium where the leadership team had set up a prayer labyrinth and a wailing wall—a cardboard replica of the one in Jerusalem. With each step, my crying intensified. By the time I entered the building, I was sobbing. I walked immediately to the wailing wall and crumpled to the ground, consumed with a grief I'd never felt before, one that emerged from deep within me. Immediately, I recognized this as Kristie, my seven-year-old self, finally expressing the sadness she'd had to hide since that day so long ago. I was—we were—finally grieving. And so I cried, heaved, and wailed with her.

"HE HURT ME!"

"I WAS SO SCARED!"

"I THOUGHT I WAS GOING TO DIE!"

I shouted into the empty room, giving voice to her thoughts, lifting them up to the cross that hung above the wailing wall, wanting Jesus to hear *her* . . . *our* . . . *my* pain.

Ten minutes later, I felt spent. I lay on the floor, surrounded by a mountain of Kleenex, listening to the sounds of the cafeteria staff preparing lunch in the next room. Thankfully, no one had entered the auditorium during this time. Even if someone had, I could not and would not have stopped crying. I understood this as a defining moment in my healing; I was finally feeling the grief from the trauma. In all my years of therapy I had tried to access my feelings, but I hit a wall every time. Turns out I was aiming for the wrong wall. The trick came in bringing my grief to the wailing wall, the place where I could lay my grief before Jesus. That's what my soul needed.

I would guess your soul might need the same thing. While not a trained therapist, I know that grief is a necessary response to trauma. Some trauma survivors may or may not feel guilt or shame; others will experience varying levels of anger or additional feelings. I believe we all hold grief in common— grief, the response to loss associated with our traumatic event. This could be the loss of a loved one, the loss of innocence and safety, the loss of a house or job, the loss of life as we knew it. As Trevor Hudson notes in his book *Hope Beyond Your Tears*, "Each person you see . . . sits next to his or her own pool of tears. . . . These pools remind us of the grief and losses that we have experienced through our lives" (pp. 14–15).

While we all carry grief of some kind, our ability to express it will vary. I have always admired my friends who were able to cry when they needed to. They seemed to be lighter, unburdened by grief expressed. But they do not seem to be the norm. I see many more folks who are either unwilling or unable to grieve. This can occur for social reasons. We live in a world that has goofy rules about crying when it comes to the boys and men among us. For some reason, we have collectively agreed that it's better if they don't. And really, no one—male or female—should cry in public. It makes us uncomfortable, and we don't want that. So we privatize grief to the point of inaccessibility, and we can't find our tears when we need them.

Our association of grief with pain complicates our grieving; the great majority of us are pain averse. Pain hurts, and we don't want to hurt. So to avoid the pain, we bury our grief, hoping that it will go away. When it doesn't, we turn to technology, food, alcohol, shopping, work, or any number of addictions to fill up the space and edge out the feelings. At times, we can be fooled into believing this approach has worked and we have successfully erased the grief. But truthfully, we really aren't happy. The pain remains, even though it resides deep beneath the surface.

I also expect we find grieving difficult because we worry that we are alone in our grief, that maybe God is not with us. That's clearly the notion that Mary and Martha entertain after their brother, Lazarus, dies. As soon as they see Jesus, Mary begins to berate him: "Lord, if you had been here, my brother wouldn't have died." She wanted Jesus to get there earlier, knowing he could have healed Lazarus and prevented his death. But now that Lazarus is dead, she wants Jesus to see her pain. Her brother is dead. She is grieving, and she wants Jesus to share in her pain.

And Jesus does. Our scripture passage tells us that Jesus looks and sees her tears and those of the community who have come to grieve Lazarus's death. It's not as if Mary's words suddenly snap him to attention and make him realize that everyone around him is crying. God the Son knows our pain. What I witness here is Mary speaking her truth. She states honestly her belief that Jesus could have healed her brother, but he didn't arrive in time. Now her brother is dead, and Mary grieves. That is her true story. When we speak our truth, we begin to see God's presence in our pain and our healing.

And that's exactly what happens.

Jesus begins to weep. Jesus—Son of God, Son of Man, the Messiah—begins to cry. And I wonder if this is the first time Jesus has wept over Lazarus's death. Perhaps, instead, it is Mary recognizing Jesus' grief for the first time. Now that she has been honest and shared her pain with Jesus, she can see that he is present in her pain. Her truth-telling doesn't lead to his tears; her truth-telling leads to her acknowledgment that Jesus is with her in her pain.

Earlier, I told you about the sermon I preached during session three of The Academy. I spoke my truth and shared my story of trauma and healing. With the homily's conclusion, it was time for the Eucharist. Blake, a member of the leadership team, served as the celebrant, the person who led us through the Communion service. In his gentle Southern drawl, Blake read through the liturgy for that evening. At one point he read these words:

> Remember, God of all mercy, those who suffer this day from injustice or poverty, with no place to call home. Remember those who are sick, imprisoned, or troubled, and those who face death with no one to comfort them. Remember, also, we pray . . . (*The Upper Room Worshipbook*, liturgy written by Don Saliers)

For a second, Blake paused, and so did we. The room fell silent as we waited for him to continue. Suddenly, I realized he was crying. At first, he cried softly, trying hard to regain his voice to continue with the service.

"We pray . . . We pray . . ."

Blake took a breath, trying to keep his voice steady.

"We pray," he tried again. "We pray . . . for women and children who have suffered violence." He began to sob. There, standing at the altar, his hands raised over the Communion elements, Blake wept.

I didn't know what to do. I felt responsible, knowing my story of trauma had led to this. Still, that moment was sacred, filled with power and profound beauty. Aside from Blake's crying, the room was completely silent. Outside, a dark, cold January day brooded. Inside, the room glowed with the light of the candles and the warmth of our communal bond.

Once he could speak again, Blake continued with the liturgy. When the appropriate time came, I joined him at the altar to help distribute the elements. He offered the bread while I held the grape juice. Placing the bread in the first person's hand, Blake began to weep again as he said, "Body of Christ, broken for you." That choked me up, so that I could only mouth the words, "Blood of Christ, shed for you." One by one, we shared Christ's sacrifice of love with each member of our community.

With the service over, the room cleared as everyone left for dinner. It was then that I knelt at the altar and began to weep—deep, heaving sobs reminiscent of my time before the wailing wall, but these tears expressed my gratitude, exhaustion, and relief. Linda, the spiritual director, came and stood beside me, her hand placed lightly on my shoulder as she prayed. I stood and hugged her.

"I can't get over Blake's tears!" I said, still trying to process what had happened.

She smiled. "I think that was Jesus. You were seeing Jesus crying for you, the way he did all those years ago when you were traumatized."

She was right. I was dumbfounded. I hadn't even considered that.

The next morning, I went to Blake and hugged him. "Thank you for last night—the way you led the liturgy and shared your tears. I was so touched," I said. "Linda suggested that you may have been the tears of Christ for me, which is so profound."

"Here's what you need to know," he responded, looking directly into my eyes. "As soon as you finished your sermon, I could feel the tears forming, but I fought them back. Then, as I was praying through the liturgy, I kept feeling the tears, but I wanted to get through the service. When I finally reached that point in the liturgy where we offer up our own prayers, I knew I wanted to say, 'we pray for women and children who have suffered violence.' I knew I was going to say that, and that's when I began to cry. And as I wept, I heard a voice say, 'These are our tears.'"

I stared at him.

"*Our* tears!" he repeated. "I couldn't believe it! That's when I knew I needed to get out of the way. I was just the vessel for these tears and shouldn't try to stop them. So I cried holy tears—the tears of God the Father, God the Son, and God the Holy Spirit"

If you doubt that God exists to comfort you in your trauma, then let this story of holy tears wash it away. God is not distant and uncaring. God is right here with you, grieving—sobbing, even—for you and the pain you have endured. God is grieved with and for you and wants only to comfort and hold you. Isaiah 53:4 reads, "Surely he hath borne our griefs, and carried our sorrows" (KJV). You do not have to carry this grief by yourself any longer. You can share it with God, who is strong enough to bear it *for* you and share in it *with* you. Together, you may weep and wail and give voice to your feelings until you can find your way out of the darkness.

Come, and enter into the holy tears.

REFLECTION QUESTIONS

1. Have you been able to grieve and share your tears with God? If not, what has prevented you from doing so? What would help you grieve?
2. What can serve as your wailing wall? Who or what can offer a safe place for you to bring your grief before Jesus?
3. In the scripture passage, Mary had the opportunity to confront Jesus and share her feelings. What do you have to say to Jesus?
4. What other places in the Bible indicate that God grieves with us?
5. Have you noticed signs around you that Jesus grieves with you? If so, what are they? If you have not experienced Jesus' sharing in your pain, what would help you do that?
6. What grief do you need to share with Jesus?
7. Kristen described physical signs in her body that pointed her to the grief within her. What signs do you notice in your body? What is your body telling you?

Prayer Bead Experience

Cross: God of grace,
Invitatory bead: heal my spirit
Resurrection bead: by the power of your Son, Jesus Christ.
1ˢᵗ cruciform bead: Listen as I describe my grief.
Week beads, set 1: Use each bead to describe your grief to God—what it looks like, feels like, sounds like, and so on.
2ⁿᵈ cruciform bead: Hear me as I tell you the impact this grief has had on me.
Week beads, set 2: Use each bead to state the effects this grief has had on your life.
3ʳᵈ cruciform bead: Help me to recognize that you are grieving with me.
Week beads, set 3: Use each bead to consider times in your life when you may have seen signs that God grieves with you. If you cannot remember any such times, use each bead to ask for help in identifying these signs.
4ᵗʰ cruciform bead: Knowing that you are present and sharing in my pain, I ask you to heal my grief.
Week beads, set 4: Use each bead to pray for healing and to recognize that God is present in your pain.
Resurrection bead: In the name of Jesus Christ,
Invitatory bead: who has the power to heal me.
Cross: Amen.

Listening Focus

Jesus weeps with me.

What Do You Notice?

What insights, feelings, memories, or other wisdom arose as you read the chapter material or completed the prayer bead experience? Whom can you share this with?

Take a minute to use your prayer beads to connect with your body. Sit quietly and breathe deeply with each bead. As you do, stay present in the moment, releasing any concerns, anxiety, or distractions. Embrace this place of stillness with God before you continue in your journey.

ANGER

Jonah thought this was utterly wrong, and he became angry. He prayed to the LORD, "Come on, LORD! Wasn't this precisely my point when I was back in my own land? This is why I fled to Tarshish earlier! I know that you are a merciful and compassionate God, very patient, full of faithful love, and willing not to destroy. At this point, LORD, you may as well take my life from me, because it would be better for me to die than to live.

The LORD responded, "Is your anger a good thing?"

—JONAH 4:1-4

TRUTH-TELLING

During the plenary for session six of The Academy we were meeting with Sister Kathleen Flood. I raised my hand to speak these words.

Sister, I'm a survivor of childhood trauma, and for most of my life I believed God had abandoned me during that time. I didn't understand why God hadn't flown me to safety or prevented the trauma when I knew God was capable of doing so. But through my healing journey, I've come to understand that God never abandoned me. God was with me during the trauma as well as in every moment afterward. I know for sure that God is always with me.

But this is where it leaves me: I don't know what to pray for. When we send our children off to school, we pray that God will keep them safe. But then there are school shootings, and children die. When loved ones are going on a trip, we pray that God will grant them a safe journey. But then car accidents and plane crashes happen.

So I'm left wondering what to pray for. I don't believe for a second that God causes school shootings or plane crashes. But God is not preventing these things from happening. Thus, it doesn't make sense to me to pray for someone's safe journey or to pray for my son's safety when he goes to school. What, then, should I pray for?"

Sister Kathleen sat quietly for a long time, pondering the question. Carefully, she said,

> I don't know. I don't know the answer to that question. I'll have to think about it for a while, but I will say that we pray to let God know what's on our heart. We want our children to be safe and for people to arrive safely at their destinations. We want people to be cured from cancer and for wars and famines to end. That doesn't always happen, but it is what we desperately want. Perhaps, we pray these prayers to share our hopes and fears and know that God hears us. We pray these prayers knowing God wants these things too so the praying is a way of uniting our hearts with God's. And I also feel we pray that people know God's presence at all times, particularly in the hard times. So when bad things do happen, we have God's promise that God is with the children in the school or the people in the plane crash, comforting, strengthening, and carrying them and us. So maybe that's what we pray for.

I wasn't disappointed in Sister Kathleen's response. It was helpful. And I knew there was no way for her to answer my question, but it was important for me and my healing to ask it. As trauma survivors, we have lots of questions. We have endured pain and heartache, and it's not fair. We did not deserve these awful things, and we want to know why they happened. We want to know who's responsible and what this means for our lives. In particular, we want to know where God is in all of this. Because while the answers are important, what we truly want is a place to focus our anger and rage. We are angry about what happened to us. We are angry at the situation, angry at the people involved, angry about the damage, angry at God. We are angry. And we need to be able to express that.

This chapter was one of the last I wrote. I wasn't sure what to say about anger. It's not that I haven't struggled with anger. Trust me, I have. I have thrown holy fits over small things: a hanger getting caught up in my closet, the seatbelt in my car getting stuck, another car cutting in front of me while driving. These small things unleashed a stream of cuss words, door slamming, and punches to the air that made it clear I had an anger problem.

For the most part, no one was around to witness these tantrums; it's a good thing, because I felt enough shame about them on my own. But a few times bystanders were present, increasing the odds of collateral damage. The worst took place when Matthew was about four years old. We were in the bathroom brushing his teeth before school. He and I were arguing about something. Like both of his parents, Matthew is headstrong and stubborn, and I knew I was getting nowhere with him. I don't remember the subject of the argument, but I was getting very frustrated. Holding the glass he used to rinse, I set it down hard on the counter, causing it to shatter. I remember the look of surprise and fear on his little face. I knew instantly I had let my anger get out of control. I was heartbroken. This was in 2009, the year my prayers for peace had reached fever pitch.

Aside from these outbursts, I channeled my anger primarily in seeking justice. The positive side to this came in my involvement in social justice issues. Not surprisingly, I spent my career fighting for people who had been victimized, treated unjustly, or neglected. I started by volunteering in a domestic violence shelter in college. That led to jobs in the areas of juvenile justice, sexual assault, and disability rights over an eighteen-year period. These jobs gave me the chance to use the power of my anger for good. Where I had been robbed of the chance to speak up and receive justice, I helped others find their voices, pursue their cases, and experience closure. I loved this work and felt a great sense of satisfaction in working with others to heal their wounds and make the world a little brighter for all of us.

But the downside to my need for justice sometimes got the better of me. It didn't take much for me to get worked up when a situation wasn't just. I couldn't abide it when someone got away with something, whether it was breaking the rules, harming another person, or generally creating drama in a relationship or organization. I wanted the rule-breakers or drama-creators to be confronted. I wanted those people to see the error of their ways, repent, and make things right. It didn't matter if it was in my job or the church (aka my husband's job), our family or friends. I. wanted. justice.

You see where this is going, don't you? It wasn't always pretty. Though I had good intentions, many times I had just enough self-righteousness to be dangerous, interfering in matters that did not involve me. Feeling a little too powerful, getting overly invested, focusing a little too much on judgment and vindication. And in the off chance that I recognized the inappropriate nature of my stepping in or the situation was such that I couldn't get involved, I would get worked up. I would obsess and lose sleep, knowing I wasn't going to see things made right (as I saw them). It wasn't healthy.

That seems to be what's going on here in our scripture passage. The prophet Jonah has not had an easy time. We may be familiar with the first part of his story: God calls him to go to the city of Nineveh and warn the inhabitants that God is going to destroy them because of their evil ways. Jonah doesn't want to do it. Instead, he flees on a boat to Tarshish (the opposite direction); God sends a storm to slow him down. The sailors on the boat panic, but Jonah admits that the storm is his fault and encourages the sailors to throw him overboard to ensure their safety. So they do. And Jonah gets swallowed by a great fish, where he hangs out for three days, praying and repenting to God, before being spit out onto dry land. God tells Jonah again to go to Nineveh, and this time he obeys. He walks through the city, preaching and warning the Ninevites to repent. And they do; they listen and ask for forgiveness and change their ways. God sees this, has mercy on them, and decides to spare the city of Nineveh.

Jonah gets really mad about this turn of events. As our passage reads, he thinks this is "utterly wrong." He can't believe the Lord is going to forgive these evildoers. What about God's promise to smite them? These people were wrong, and God promised to punish them. They were going to be judged and get what was coming to them. Do bad, and bad things will happen to you. That's the way the world works. Right?

Right? You and I know that's not true. And it's why I believe many of us struggle with anger.

This is as good a place as any to deal with the problem of evil in the world. And by evil, I mean all the reasons we gather around this book: violence, abuse, natural disasters, suicide, combat, car crashes, betrayals, death, and all the other events that cause us harm of any kind. Why do these bad things happen to us? Why does God let evil things happen? Is evil God's way of punishing us? There are questions. So many questions.

Unfortunately, no good answers exist. We do not know why God permits evil to exist in the world. We do not know why bad things happen to good people. We do not know why God doesn't intervene in every situation. We do not know. Humans have struggled with this problem since the dawn of time; entire forests have been leveled to print the books written about this problem; Google brings up 88,500,000 results when you type in "problem of evil." Everyone is searching, but no one knows.

That's not to say God has remained silent on the subject. Indeed, God has a lot to say about evil and injustice, as evidenced by the crucifixion. As Jesus hangs nailed to a cross, a crown of thorns on his head, God takes on evil with everything God has—the fullness of divine love in Jesus and his willingness to die for the sake of Creation. This is an act of complete grace rather than vengeance: Jesus does not die to satisfy a vengeful God. Instead, God the Son willingly takes on sin to prevent sin from destroying us. This scene on the cross is the crux of God's answer to the problem of evil, though it does not end there. There is more.

During Sunday worship, many Christians traditionally recite the Apostles' Creed. This ancient creed offers a concise summary of the Christian faith. At one point we proclaim what we believe about Jesus by saying,

> who was crucified, died, and was buried;
> he descended into hell.
> On the third day he rose again.

Growing up in the Presbyterian church, I always wondered what that second line meant. Did Jesus really go to hell? By adulthood I had joined The United Methodist Church where that line was stripped out. Elaine Heath, one of our faculty for session seven and a fellow trauma survivor, criticized this omission, arguing the significance of proclaiming that Jesus went to hell. For many of us, hell is the place where evil rules and all the bad people go, so in this act we see that God's grace reaches every place and everyone; no place on earth or in heaven or hell lies outside God's grace and redeeming love; there is no place where evil remains in control. Love trumps evil. Always and everywhere.

More importantly, Elaine argued that as trauma survivors we have been to hell. We have personally experienced times when we felt like we were in hell; certainly, our traumatic experiences were, themselves, forms of hell. That's why she insists this second line is fundamental to our healing: We need to know that God's justice will be comprehensive and complete. We need to know that God will wipe out evil even to the ends of hell. We need to know that justice will reign and that we will be vindicated. Then, come Easter, we can truly celebrate the Resurrection.

I understand those assurances may not be enough right now. You want to know when and how you will be vindicated. You want justice *now*. No wonder you are angry. No wonder you have had it with God. After what you've experienced, justice seems like a simple request. But so far, it seems like you've heard nothing but crickets. I get it. And so do many, many others.

The best I can offer is this: First, make sure your anger is "a good thing," as God said to Jonah. This is not to question the validity of your anger. You have every reason to be angry, and it's crucial to your healing journey that you express it. But use your anger to move forward rather than backward in your recovery and advocate for yourself and others. Don't be like Jonah— willing to die rather than live because of your anger. You can easily allow your anger to consume you; unexpressed anger can lead to heart attacks, severe depression, uncontrolled rage, addictions, and many other detrimental conditions. Don't let that happen. Instead, find healthy options to express and release your anger, such as therapy, yoga, exercise, journaling, prayer, or creative activities. I worked at a rape crisis center that held plate-smashing parties—safe spaces where survivors and volunteers could channel their rage and pain into a plate, then hurl it against a brick wall. It felt great! Then we gathered up the shattered pieces and used them to create gorgeous mosaic tables, picture frames, and planters.

Second, know you are not alone; all of us feel or have felt the same way. You are not alone because God is with you even in your anger. Indeed, God wants to share in your anger, to hear it and feel it. God can handle it.

As we see time and time again from the Psalms, it is okay—healthy even—to rage against God. In the raging we acknowledge God's presence. (Otherwise, who are we yelling at?) In our ranting we give words to our feelings, releasing them rather than keeping them caged up. Our raving moves us forward in our journey toward healing. If you need any encouragement, read Psalms 22; 88; or 137 for good examples of folks who unleashed their anger on God.

Sister Kathleen wasn't able to give me the answer I sought, but that's okay. Her response was exactly what I needed. She received my question with sincerity and respect. She didn't offer empty platitudes or pat answers to fill the space, and she didn't dismiss me or make me feel crazy. She gave me room to voice my question, then joined me in the awkward space that followed. And that's what I needed: companionship in the place that held my need, anger, confusion, and hope. Because that's a sacred place. And surely God is in that place.

REFLECTION QUESTIONS

1. What are you angry about?
2. How do you express your anger? Which are healthy ways? Which are unhealthy?
3. Do you identify with Jonah in the scripture passage? Why or why not?
4. What questions do you have for God?
5. What do you think about the problem of evil? How does this impact your understanding of what happened to you?
6. If you were to write a psalm, what would it sound like?
7. What do you need to heal your anger?

PRAYER BEAD EXPERIENCE

Cross: God of grace,

Invitatory bead: heal my spirit

Resurrection bead: by the power of your Son, Jesus Christ.

1st cruciform bead: Listen as I describe my anger.

Week beads, set 1: Use each bead to describe your feelings of anger to God—what it looks like, feels like, sounds like, and so on.

2nd cruciform bead: Hear me as I tell you the impact this feeling of anger has had on me.

Week beads, set 2: Use each bead to share how this anger has affected your life.

3rd cruciform bead: Help me to bring my questions to you, trusting that you will receive and honor them.

Week beads, set 3: Use each bead to lift your questions to God. What do you struggle with? What explanations do you need?

4th cruciform bead: Heal me of my anger.

Week beads, set 4: Use each bead to pray for healing and to know that God can handle your anger.

Resurrection bead: In the name of Jesus Christ,

Invitatory bead: who has the power to heal me.

Cross: Amen.

Listening Focus

Hear my anger, Lord.

What Do You Notice?

What insights, feelings, memories, or other wisdom arose as you read the chapter material or completed the prayer bead experience? Whom can you share this with?

Take a minute to use your prayer beads to connect with your body. Sit quietly and breathe deeply with each bead. As you do, stay present in the moment, releasing any concerns, anxiety, or distractions. Embrace this place of stillness with God before you continue in your journey.

ABANDONMENT

The LORD said to Moses: Speak to the Israelites and say to them: Make fringes on the edges of your clothing for all time. Have them put blue cords on the fringe on the edges. This will be your fringe. You will see it and remember all the LORD's commands and do them. Then you won't go exploring the lusts of your own heart or your eyes. In this way you'll remember to do all my commands. Then you will be holy to your God. I am the LORD your God, who brought you out of the land of Egypt to be your God. I am the LORD your God.

—NUMBERS 15:37-41

TRUTH-TELLING

There are no words to describe how it felt to be seven years old, traumatized, and having to suck it up and keep quiet about it. But abandonment might be a good place to start. My life was shattered; my childhood, my innocence, my sense of wonder and security—instantly gone. And I had no one to comfort me. No one to weep with me. No one to tell me this wasn't my fault. No one to seek justice on my behalf.

And where was God in all of this? Why had God allowed this to happen to me—a bright, spunky, little girl with a pixie cut and a love of Barbies and Donny Osmond? Why hadn't God rescued me? Surely, God could have reached down and picked me up and flown me to safety. But God didn't.

Yeah, I'd say I felt abandoned.

Like everything else, I forced this sense of abandonment underground with all my other feelings. Only when I went to college did the feelings begin to leak out. On my own for the first time, trying to figure out who I was in the world, I started to deal with other issues in my life. Like everyone else, I had other baggage, primarily in the form of family dysfunction; so being away from home gave me the space to process this. For the first time in my life, I was feeling my feelings. Like a toddler learning to walk, I felt awkward, flailing around, pinging from one feeling to the next. Everything was new, intense, and revelatory. I sought the help of a therapist—the first of many throughout my life.

It wasn't easy. I had a lot of anger and grief. And while I could tap into feelings about my family history, I couldn't access any of the feelings related to the trauma. I had done such a good job of burying them that they were inaccessible. By now, I'd forgotten the location of my super-duper, totally awesome hiding place. Plus, family stuff was more recent and less traumatic, so I found it easier to access. But it provided good training as I learned how to process my life experiences. It was a start.

During this time I began to connect with my sense of abandonment. I couldn't *feel* it, but I could *sense* it. I had entered college with plans to go into ministry. Everything had led to this plan. I had been a leader of my high school youth group. I was ordained as our church's first youth elder. I had been a member of my presbytery's youth council. I wanted to be exactly like my youth director and follow in her footsteps. I was going to go to seminary and minister to youth and bring glory to God. So I went to Trinity University—a good Presbyterian school—and majored in religion. But by the time I graduated I had stopped going to church, ditched my plans for ministry, and distanced myself from God altogether. God had abandoned me, I reasoned, so I would abandon God.

Nineteen years later, while sitting in a Starbucks, I finally realized God had never abandoned me. It was 2008. Curled up on a chaise in the corner, sipping my chai latte, I was reading *The Shack* by William Paul Young while waiting to pick up my son from preschool. I had reached the part where Mack talks with Jesus about the abduction of his daughter, Missy. Mack struggles with the fact that his six-year-old girl had been alone to deal with an incomprehensible situation.

Gently Jesus speaks, "Mack, she was never alone. I never left her; we never left her not for one instant. I could no more abandon her, or you, than I could abandon myself. . . . There was not a moment that we were not with her" (p. 173).

In the corner of a busy Starbucks, amidst the noise of the baristas filling orders and friends gathering to chat, I began to sob. A deep cry emerged from that hiding space and shook my body. I was grateful for this release, even as I hid behind my book and tried not to cause a scene. I wept, realizing for the first time that God had been with me in that storage closet long ago, curled up with me, holding me, weeping with me, giving me the strength to endure. God had not abandoned me.

That was the first lesson.

The second came in my sermon preparation for session three of The Academy. I had chosen to preach about abandonment and knew I would use the passage from Numbers. I had first encountered that passage when I started to lead prayer bead workshops. As I talked about how other faiths used prayer beads, I showed people a Jewish prayer shawl, which has knotted fringe. Though the fringe differs from beads, I made the connection between the two because the small, round, hard knots are meant to be rolled through your fingers like the beads are in prayer. The Numbers passage is the point where God tells the Israelites to take the fringe and use it to remember God. Every time I taught, I would read that passage. And every time I missed the point.

But in the months leading up to my time in The Academy, I'd begun to recognize what was really going on in this passage. The meaning had begun to seep into my bones, until one day it occurred to me that this passage was about abandonment. Just look at what's going on with the Israelites at this point in the story: They'd been traveling across a desert from Egypt to the Promised Land. But it wasn't a direct path; they'd been wandering and going in circles and taking side trips. For forty years, y'all. Not surprisingly, they'd begun to lose hope of ever making it to the Promised Land. They were hot and tired and hungry; they were scared and angry and grieved. They worried that God had abandoned them in the wilderness. So they began to rebel: They broke the commandments, created idols, and argued with God. And God sensed their unrest.

That's when God decided to intervene. Not that God hadn't before. Just before this passage, in Numbers 6, God took the time to offer the Israelites a divine blessing:

The Lord bless you and keep you.
The Lord make his face to shine upon you, and be gracious to you;
The Lord lift up his countenance upon you, and give you peace.

This blessing satisfied the Israelites for a while. They didn't feel quite so abandoned. But eventually, after more years in the desert, the Israelites forgot the blessing and went back to feeling abandoned.

So in chapter 15, God tells Moses to pass along a message to the people. And the message is, in essence, "Hey, I hear you. I see your pain. And I want to help you. So here's some fringe."

Ummm, really? Seriously? I've been wandering in this desert and feel hopeless and scared, and you give me fringe?

But indeed, it is the perfect gift, as any gift from God would be. For God knows the Israelites' limitations. The Holy One knows that despite divine promises, interventions, and personal blessings, the Israelites are human—struggling humans in the middle of the desert. They, as physical beings, need something concrete to hold on to. As much as they want to have faith in a God they cannot see, at times they desire a tangible object that reminds them of God's presence with them. So God commands them to add fringe to their garments. Everyone would have access to it. Everyone could participate in this seemingly minor act and be reminded of God's presence. God had never abandoned them.

In 2009 while vacationing in the mountains of North Carolina, my family stopped for dinner at Salty Dog's, a fun, cheesy little seafood restaurant and biker bar combo in Maggie Valley. After dinner, we walked out of the restaurant, my husband and son ahead of me, already out the door. As I walked through the lobby, I distinctly heard a voice say, "You need to make rosaries." *Huh*, I thought, *how strange*. And I kept walking.

For the next several days, I considered that voice. It had been so clear. And aside from the fact that it came from a biker bar, it kind of made sense. For more than twenty years, I had collected rosaries, though they never did anything more than hang on my wall. I never used them to pray. I didn't pray much at all given my lack of trust in God. The voice also made sense because I had a master of theological studies—all this seminary training—that I wasn't putting to use. And I was rather crafty. I don't want to brag, but I can hold my own in a room full of basket weavers. Still, I'd never made a set of prayer beads.

But I decided to trust the voice. I began doing research, and that's when I learned about Protestant prayer beads and realized that's what this calling was about. That led to making and selling beads and leading workshops and writing books. Many of you know about that part. But it also led to my relationship with The Upper Room and Johnny Sears and The Academy, where I would finally experience the healing that only stillness with God could bring.

I was recalling the voice and its impact with my husband, Max, after session two. "How amazing," I said, "that I thought I was going to The Academy to explore my calling to make prayer beads, but it's ending up being more about my healing."

Max started laughing.

"What's so funny?" I asked.

"You don't see it, do you?" he inquired.

"What?" I asked.

"That voice at Salty Dog's—the one that told you to make rosaries — that was your fringe moment. That was God reaching out and offering you the prayer beads, something to hold on to so that you would know once and for all that God had never abandoned you. Not when you were seven, not now, not ever. That was God's breadcrumb leading you to The Academy where you would find healing and understand that God *is* with you."

What immediately popped into my mind was the day I arrived to begin The Academy and walked into the lobby of Camp Sumatanga for the first time. Across from the front desk was a large framed picture of Creel Chapel, a beautiful outdoor chapel located on top of Chandler Mountain overlooking the camp. Instantly, I realized I had a photo of that very same chapel in my family photo albums at home. The photo was of me and my mom. Apparently, we had been here when I was about four or five years old. Unbeknownst to me, God had been preparing me for what was to come, for this journey back to Sumatanga, back to the knowledge of God's presence with me. God was and always had been with me.

That was my second lesson.

Now I move with the confidence of one who has never been and never will be abandoned by God. God was with me in the awful, scary storage closet when I was seven. God was with me as I struggled to manage the aftermath of that trauma all by myself. God has been with me through the years as I struggled to deal with the damage. God has guided me through to this place of healing. God will continue to be with me every second of every day of my life. God is as close to me as the clothes on my body and the beads between my fingers.

I know this much is true.

Since you are reading this book, it is likely that you have, or someone you love has, struggled with a sense of abandonment at one time or another. Indeed, I believe it's part of the human condition. Whether it's due to violence or other trauma, divorce or the death of a loved one, lost jobs, being told we are not good enough, or been rejected for who we are, we have all plumbed the depths of despair and wondered where God was.

But hopefully we have all had our fringe moments as well—those times when divine light breaks through the darkness to remind us that God is with us. Those times when God uses common, ordinary, everyday objects like fringe or beads to reach us. Those times when God uses common, ordinary, everyday times like sitting in a Starbucks or driving to the grocery store to get our attention. Those times when God uses common, ordinary, everyday people to offer words of wisdom and grace to us. "I am the LORD your God" reads Isaiah 41:13. *I am.* God was, is, and has always been.

We are never alone. Yes, bad things happen and evil exists in the world, but God is always with us. We have never been abandoned.

Go, and see that God is with you.

REFLECTION QUESTIONS

1. When have you felt abandoned in your life?
2. Whom did you feel abandoned you?
3. What do you want to say to God about your feelings of abandonment?
4. Have you had fringe moments in your life: common, ordinary, everyday signs/objects/places/people that reveal that God is with you and has never abandoned you? If so, what did they look like?
5. What would assure you of God's presence with you?
6. What difference will it make to know that God is and has always been with you?
7. What does it mean that God was with you even in the midst of your trauma?

PRAYER BEAD EXPERIENCE

Cross: God of grace,
Invitatory bead: heal my spirit
Resurrection bead: by the power of your Son, Jesus Christ.
1st cruciform bead: Listen as I describe my sense of abandonment.
Week beads, set 1: Use each bead to describe to God your sense of abandonment—what it looks like, feels like, sounds like, and so on.
2nd cruciform bead: Hear me as I tell you what impact this feeling of abandonment has had on me.
Week beads, set 2: Use each bead to share how this sense of abandonment has affected you.
3rd cruciform bead: Help me to recognize my own fringe moments.
Week beads, set 3: Use each bead to consider your own fringe moments—those common, everyday signs/objects/places/people that point to God's abiding presence with you.
4th cruciform bead: Heal me of this sense of abandonment so I can know with certainty that you are with me.
Week beads, set 4: Use each bead to pray for healing and to know that God is with you.
Resurrection bead: In the name of Jesus Christ,
Invitatory bead: who has the power to heal me.
Cross: Amen.

Listening Focus

God is with me.

What Do You Notice?

What insights, feelings, memories, or other wisdom arose as you read the chapter material or completed the prayer bead experience? Whom can you share this with?

Take a minute to use your prayer beads to connect with your body. Sit quietly and breathe deeply with each bead. As you do, stay present in the moment, releasing any concerns, anxiety, or distractions. Embrace this place of stillness with God before you continue in your journey.

SHAME

Jesus went to the Mount of Olives. Early in the morning he returned to the temple. All the people gathered around him, and he sat down and taught them. The legal experts and Pharisees brought a woman caught in adultery. Placing her in the center of the group, they said to Jesus, "Teacher, this woman was caught in the act of committing adultery. In the Law, Moses commanded us to stone women like this. What do you say?" They said this to test him, because they wanted a reason to bring an accusation against him. Jesus bent down and wrote on the ground with his finger.

They continued to question him, so he stood up and replied, "Whoever hasn't sinned should throw the first stone." Bending down again, he wrote on the ground. Those who heard him went away, one by one, beginning with the elders. Finally, only Jesus and the woman were left in the middle of the crowd.

Jesus stood up and said to her, "Woman, where are they? Is there no one to condemn you?"

She said, "No one, sir."

Jesus said, "Neither do I condemn you. Go, and from now on, don't sin anymore."

—JOHN 8:1-11

TRUTH-TELLING

When I was eight years old I spent a lot of time apologizing to people. Whether it was something major or the tiniest of infractions, I would constantly say "I'm sorry" at the drop of a hat. I don't know for sure, but I'm guessing I even said it for things I wasn't responsible for. I do know that I said it so much that one day my mom actually banned me from saying "I'm sorry."

"You say it so much, it no longer has meaning," she explained.

I found this perplexing. My mom had raised us to be polite. We were good about offering up thank-yous and pleases at the appropriate times and, yes, even apologizing when necessary. Now she was telling me not to do it.

She was right, of course. Apologizing had become a mindless habit. The ban served a useful purpose: It forced me to stop and consider my actions and words. I had to come up with new ways to acknowledge my mistakes and, more significantly, make sure I meant what I said; no more empty words. The lesson got my attention and has stayed with me all these years.

This story comes to mind because I can look back and see how just one year after the assault, shame and guilt were already an integral part of my life, so much so that they had infused my behavior and words. I had moved beyond apologizing for the various mistakes I made as a kid to apologizing for the trauma itself. In my eight-year-old mind, I was responsible for the assault. *I* was the one who had agreed to walk away with the bicycle guy, a choice that had led to unimaginable consequences. My family had even been threatened. Not only had my decision hurt me deeply, but it put my mom and little brother at risk. I believe I kept apologizing because no amount of "I'm sorrys" could erase what I had done. I was guilty. I was bad. I was shameful.

It's no wonder I had reached this point. The bicycle guy had made sure of that by threatening me into silence. Robbed of the ability to speak my truth and have others comfort me and tell me it wasn't my fault, I had no other choice but to absorb the experience and the feelings that came with it. I was too young to understand that the guilt lay with him. At seven years of age, I didn't know what to make of it and could only assume I was responsible for what had happened and that what had happened made me a bad person.

This is clearly when the perfectionist in me was born, because from then on, I worked with every fiber of my being to undo the damage I had done. I didn't want to be a bad person, so I made excellent grades, stayed out of trouble (as best a kid could), tried to be helpful, and looked for opportunities to prove my worth. I became focused, driven, ambitious—working hard to hide my shame. Not surprisingly, this didn't always work, and any crack in the facade sent me reeling, vexing me and forcing me to double down at damage control. Even as I achieved success in adulthood, each success brought more pressure to perform even better than before, to stay one step ahead of the shame nipping at my heels. I should note that perfectionism wasn't my only shame defense; I also used food and shopping to hide and numb.

The real problem here is that my shame got in the way of my relationships with others and particularly with Jesus. I didn't believe there was any way God would want to hang out with someone as shameful as me. There was no way God could love me. I was damaged goods, and I felt pretty sure God was not in the business of damaged goods. Of course, I had that all wrong. Though God does not see anyone as damaged goods, God is certainly in the business of helping people who feel they are. We have only to look at the stories of Jesus to see that, including the one in this scripture passage.

In their continued effort to trap Jesus and gather reasons to arrest him, the legal experts bring to him a woman who has been caught having an affair. The issue for them is that she has broken the law, and they want to see what Jesus will do in this situation. Will he agree with them and condemn her? Or will he do something, you know, Jesus-like?

Aside from the fact that she has broken the law, you can imagine the scorn they have for this woman. I'm sure they were physically rough in their handling of her, called her names, spoke derisively of her, and even reveled in the thought of stoning her. You can hear it in their words as they refer to her as one of "women like this." She is no longer a person in their eyes. They have expanded her guilt related to an action and used it to describe her entire being. She is shameful, unworthy of compassion, forgiveness, or even life.

Brené Brown explains that our culture commonly links shame and guilt. When we hear that someone has done something wrong, our perception of that person changes. We associate the person with his/her action. But shame and guilt are not the same thing. According to Brown, guilt comes in thinking *I did something bad*, whereas shame is concluding *I am bad* (p. 71). That was the case for me. I believed I had done something wrong and was therefore a bad person. Obviously that's part of what's going on in this passage: The legal experts have declared this woman shameful; perhaps she believed that of herself. But Jesus isn't buying it.

Jesus challenges the men, suggesting that the one who has never sinned be the first to throw a stone. Every one of them has sinned; not one of them is perfect. So, one by one, they drop their stones and walk away.

It's here that Jesus turns to her and says, "Woman, where are they?" Did you catch that? He calls her "woman." He doesn't say "adulterer" or "shameful person." He reinstates her personhood, the identity the men have tried to erase. Jesus treats her with respect and reinforces the idea that the woman is not her condition. She is not her actions. She is not a woman "like this." She is not shameful. She is worthy of the Lord's compassion, forgiveness, and deep love. That is her true self. That is our true self: people created by God and worthy of God's deep love no matter what. Our goal is to reclaim this truth.

It's telling that after eating the apple in the garden of Eden, one of the first feelings Adam and Eve experience is shame. Where previously they have been naked—vulnerable—and okay with this; now their nakedness embarrasses them. They have no way to cover up the reality of their disobedience. They are completely exposed and ashamed, making it clear that now shame is part of the human condition.

In their desire to hide their shame, Adam and Eve hide from God and use fig leaves to cover up their private parts. During session seven of The Academy, Elaine Heath explained that fig leaves are irritating to the skin. They can even cause severe skin reactions, including horrible rashes. Not only does it come naturally to us to feel shame and want to hide from it; it also seems to be human nature to want to punish ourselves when we feel shame! Whether through criticism, addiction, self-harm, or other ways, we always seem to find ways to castigate ourselves.

Lucky for us, we serve a God who loves us deeply, who does not accept that we are our shame and does not want us to suffer for it. Thus, God calls to Adam and Eve, desiring to be with them. When they don't respond, God continues to call, eventually wooing them from their hiding place. Next, God gives Adam and Eve real clothes to wear, ones that will not cause pain. What an act of mercy! Rather than passing judgment, God ministers to Adam and Eve in the midst of their shame. It is one of the first encounters of God's grace following the forbidden fruit-eating incident. We should take this seriously. God does not punish and shame us, nor does God want us to punish ourselves. God is not in the business of shame. We shouldn't be either.

I realize this is easier said than done. Shame seems to come naturally to us. Like a virus, it enters our system without our awareness, gradually expanding and taking over our subconscious self until it is too late. Where once stood a confident person, assured of her place in the world, now there stands someone who hides and cowers and apologizes for taking up space in the universe, so sure is she that she is forever tainted by her life experiences. Shame has become so much a part of her that she accepts as true the lies that shame tells her: *You are not worthy. This is as good as it gets. Don't even bother.*

You are a mess. At times, these lies may come from other people wanting to shame us. But we must not listen to the lies. We must remain focused on God who continually whispers that we are God's beloved, chosen to bear God's sacred image, and called to live lives full of grace. We are truly God's delight.

Ignoring the lies and accepting our worth takes immense trust—in ourselves and in God. Though God tries at every turn to remind us of our value, we can easily miss the signs or fail to hear the whispers, particularly when our own internal record plays the song of our shame and judgment loudly and constantly. That's where the practice of the prayer beads or journaling can help.

Throughout my life I have tried to journal on a regular basis. I know it's good for me spiritually, emotionally, and otherwise. Plus, I'm a writer, and all the best writers talk about journaling as a necessary part of the calling. So I would buy a new journal (the best part of the whole process). I would write in it every day for about two weeks. Then I would begin to avoid it, writing less frequently. I would think, *I really should write that down in my journal.* Or worse, *I'm supposed to be writing in my journal.* And just as quickly I would say, *Nah,* and pursue another activity. Eventually, that journal would make it to the top shelf of my studio to be added to my collection of about twenty journals, each of which is about one-sixth complete.

I believe I found journaling a hard practice because of my shame. The page seemed to taunt me. But everyone on my team—my therapist, my spiritual director, and folks in The Academy—encouraged me to journal, and so I did. Not every day, of course, but at least on a somewhat regular basis. I specifically journaled about the night terrors. I wrote about when they happened, what my thoughts and feelings were, whether I jumped out of bed or screamed, and what the disturbance was trying to tell me. This recording helped me see the primary message of the night terrors: "I made a bad choice, and now I'm going to be killed." My night terrors continually rehearsed the birth of my shame, the moment when I chose to walk away with the bicycle guy. Seeing how that shame intrinsically connected to my fear, I felt exposed and vulnerable again, afraid of being hurt.

My journal also revealed that the night terrors always occurred on days when I felt stressed by my fear of making a mistake or disappointing someone. Didn't get all my work done? Night terror. Husband upset with me? Night terror. Too much to do? Night terror.

Perhaps I need to stop trying to be perfect, I thought, particularly since I wasn't perfect at trying to be perfect. (Who knew?) And especially since it was causing me such distress. With this realization, I decided to forgive myself. CeCe, my spiritual director, adamantly asserted that I had done nothing wrong and had no reason to forgive myself for what happened with the bicycle guy. On an intellectual level I knew she was right. But at the heart level I acknowledged that I was holding on to major grievances with myself.

So I practiced being nicer to myself. I made room for imperfection and failure, recognizing that I'm not perfect. This decision freed me; I no longer had to work overtime to be someone I was not. I could just be me. I stopped berating myself at every turn. I found opportunities to compliment myself. I took better care of myself. Granted, I was not perfect at being imperfect; some days I would get caught up in the moment and criticize myself. When that happened I simply envisioned Jesus saying, "Neither do I condemn you," and I would forgive myself. As a result, I began to release myself from shame and discovered that I actually like myself. Imagine that.

Of all the issues we experience as trauma survivors, shame may be the most difficult to address. It is subtle and pervasive, going to the core of our identity. I have known many people, from close friends and family members, to coworkers and clients, who have struggled with shame. I've watched how hard they must work to release the shame that binds them. It takes work—a lot of it, as well as time and dogged persistence. But it can be overcome.

I pray you will engage in the necessary work to erase the shame lies and declare your worthiness. I pray you will dig down to the origins of the shame, root it out, and replace it with self-love. I pray you will grow to love yourself and treat yourself with the honor you are due. I pray you will experience God's delight in you. Because you are worthy.

Imagine that.

REFLECTION QUESTIONS

1. Do you feel shame? How, where, and when do you notice it?
2. What is your shame about? What is it connected to?
3. How do you try to cover your shame?
4. What does it mean to you to affirm that you are not your condition?
5. What do you need to forgive yourself for?
6. What does it mean to you to know that God delights in you?
7. What can you do to honor yourself? to practice self-care?

PRAYER BEAD EXPERIENCE

Cross: God of grace,

Invitatory bead: heal my spirit

Resurrection bead: by the power of your Son, Jesus Christ.

1ˢᵗ cruciform bead: Listen as I describe my sense of shame.

Week beads, set 1: Use each bead to describe your sense of shame to God— what it looks like, feels like, sounds like, and so on.

2ⁿᵈ cruciform bead: Hear me as I tell you what impact this sense of shame has had on me.

Week beads, set 2: Use each bead to share how this sense of shame has affected your life.

3ʳᵈ cruciform bead: Help me to recognize that I am your child and have no need to feel shame. I am worthy.

Week beads, set 3: Use each bead to consider how you are a child of God, worthy of God's deep love.

4ᵗʰ cruciform bead: Heal me of my sense of shame so that I can know with certainty that you love me and delight in me.

Week beads, set 4: Use each bead to pray for healing and to experience God's delight in you.

Resurrection bead: In the name of Jesus Christ,

Invitatory bead: who has the power to heal me.

Cross: Amen.

Listening Focus

I am worthy. God delights in me.

What Do You Notice?

What insights, feelings, memories, or other wisdom arose as you read the chapter material or completed the prayer bead experience? Whom can you share this with?

Take a minute to use your prayer beads to connect with your body. Sit quietly and breathe deeply with each bead. As you do, stay present in the moment, releasing any concerns, anxiety, or distractions. Embrace this place of stillness with God before you continue in your journey.

FEAR

[Gabriel] said, "Don't be afraid. You are greatly treasured. All will be well with you. Be strong!"

—Daniel 10:19

Truth-Telling

With all this healing going on, I thought for sure the fear would disappear. And it did to some degree; I was getting better at trusting and being still and had many moments of joy and peace. But other symptoms signaled that the fear remained, primarily taking the form of those awful night terrors. I still screamed and leapt out of bed, a clear indication that as my mind and spirit worked to let go of fear, my body still held on to it with a death grip. I was beyond frustrated; I was downright disgusted. My desperate prayer had always focused on releasing the fear, and despite my making so much progress, the fear remained. I worried that I would never rid myself of it.

As I mentioned in the chapter on shame, I understood that the night terrors were partly related to my self-imposed guilt. That led me to wonder whether the guilt was also the basis for my fear: that in betraying myself, I had opened myself up to violence, and thus fear. If that were true, I reasoned, then forgiving myself would clear things up and all would be well. Right? Right or not, I planned to explore this premise as I entered Academy session five.

One of my fellow Academy #34 members was a man named Paul, a retired Army chaplain. Early on in our Academy experience, I had written him off precisely because of his military background. I assumed we would have nothing in common, given that I am a pacifist and generally have problems with rules and authority figures. I figured he was serious, conservative, even gruff. Was I ever wrong. Paul, it turns out, is smart, insightful, and deeply empathic, making it plain that the soldiers he supported throughout his career were in excellent hands. He is also hilarious, with a boisterous laugh that envelops the room and everyone in it. This led to the beginning of our bond. His revelation that he too is a PTSD survivor from his time in Iraq sealed our bond. By session five, we were good friends.

Paul greeted me with a bear hug on day one, and we spent the next few minutes catching up on our life between sessions. Eventually, I said, "I'm expecting this to be a tough session for me."

"Really? What's going on?"

"I sense this session is about learning to forgive myself and letting go of fear."

Paul nodded as if he understood exactly what I meant. "Gotcha. Just let me know when you need someone to listen. I'll be right here."

By midweek I began to feel that familiar heaviness in my chest; it was time to head over to the wailing wall. There I cried, confessing my need to forgive myself—to let that cute, spunky little seven-year-old off the hook and give my forty-something self a break. I experienced a true catharsis, which I shared with Paul. By the end of the day, I felt I had crossed a new threshold in my healing journey. I went to bed feeling hopeful, confident that I would sleep like a baby.

But that's not at all what happened.

Within the first hour of going to sleep, I had a night terror that sent me clear across the room. Crawling back into bed, I lay still, waiting for my heart to stop violently thumping. I couldn't believe it. Did I really just have a night disturbance after such a great day of healing? I mean, I had forgiven myself, right? What else was there to do? Why, why, why was I still having night terrors? Would I ever be rid of them? Would I ever be rid of fear?

Thirty minutes later, I received what seemed to be an answer. Having finally drifted back to sleep, I suddenly felt something on my back. It was like someone was running a finger down the length of my spine. My body shuddered impulsively, and I leapt out of bed, my heart racing faster than before. I turned on the light and looked around, convinced that someone was in the room. But I was alone. Again, I was in disbelief.

What in the world was that? That had never ever happened before. My night terrors, while a complete pain, had a distinct, familiar imprint, one that didn't involve the feeling of someone's finger running down my back.

Oh, no, I thought. *Are they getting* worse? And did this mean my fear would get worse instead of better? I started to freak out, worrying that perhaps I was losing my mind. I felt panicked and truly scared. For the rest of the night I lay flat on my back, sleeping fitfully, aware of every noise.

The next morning, Paul greeted me with a smile and hug. "Hey, buddy! I hope you slept well last night!" He read my expression and understood immediately that wasn't the case.

Later, during quiet time, he sought me out and sat with me on the porch. Though we were supposed to be silent, I was grateful for the chance to talk.

"I had the worst terror of my life," I complained.

"And you thought the night terrors would be over," he replied. "You thought you were done with all that."

I nodded as tears streamed down my face.

He offered a gentle smile. "You look at healing like it's a light switch; you should be able to just flip the switch to 'off' and there won't be any more night terrors, no more fear."

Again, I nodded.

"Problem is, healing is more like a dimmer switch." He formed a circle with his fingers as if he was adjusting a dial. "There are times when the switch is dialed one way and you have more symptoms, and there's times when the switch is the other way, and you feel pretty good."

"Does that mean I'll never be rid of the night terrors?" I couldn't bear the thought. "Am I always going to be afraid?" I started to cry again.

"I don't know. I don't believe so. But I do know that you need more time. The more time you give it, the more you heal, the more the dial turns toward good things and fewer symptoms. There still may be times when it gets nudged back a bit, but if you understand it as a process rather than an on/off switch, you won't be as worried when you have a night disturbance. You'll be able to look back over time and see the progress you've made."

"I was just so hopeful that I had come up with an answer to my fear. That I needed to forgive myself finally and all would be well."

"But look at all that's happened in the year we've been coming to The Academy. Look at all that's happened to you. That's some pretty incredible healing going on there, don't you think?"

"Yeah." I offered a weak smile. I couldn't deny the profound experiences that I had already known.

"That tells me you're on the right path and doing the right things. Just give it some more time and trust the process. Remember, it's not an on/off switch." He formed his fingers in a circle again. "It's a dimmer switch."

I thought about that dimmer switch for the rest of the session, partly because every time I saw Paul he would smile, hold up his hand, and mimic adjusting a dial. And also because I knew Paul was right: I wanted to be able to flip the switch to off and declare myself healed and fear-free. I wanted it to be simple. More than that, I wanted to have control. I wanted to be able to figure out how to heal myself, get it done, and move on. I didn't want to have to wait, and I sure didn't want to have to rely on others. Or God. I wanted to be healed now, on my time line.

But one sure thing I had learned from The Academy was to trust God. So I focused on trusting. And two things happened.

First, about a month later I was sitting in the waiting room of my therapist's office flipping through magazines. A headline on the cover of *Scientific American Mind* caught my eye: "She Hears Voices (and Actually Listens)." Turning to the story, I read about Eleanor Longden, a British woman who began hearing voices in college and was diagnosed with schizophrenia. Traditional medicine taught her to fear or distrust the voices and try to get rid of them via medication and therapy. Her condition deteriorated. But over time, Eleanor began to suspect that the voices could serve as a source of insight rather than something to fear. It was possible, she reasoned, that the voices had developed as a result of trauma and had a purpose: to alert her when she was stressed and help her identify ways to handle the stressors. So she started to trust the voices and notice when they showed up. Sure enough, their presence corresponded with stressful or fearful times. The more she noticed this, the less she feared them. Gradually, they decreased in intensity and frequency to the point that they were manageable.

Hmmm. Could the same be true with my night terrors?

I started to pay more attention to them. Following my therapist's suggestion, every time I had a night disturbance I got out of bed, sat down at my desk, and wrote in my journal. This enabled me to document the frequency of the events and use my journal to try to understand what was going on before, during, and after the night terrors. Over time, I could see how the terrors were, indeed, related to what was going on in my life. Stressful days generally ended with some type of sleep disturbance.

"When you were molested, you couldn't say anything about it because the bicycle guy threatened you," Stacey, my therapist, explained. "So your body had to absorb the trauma. And you did that for so long that over time your body learned to absorb any stress you encountered in life. But it couldn't hold on to it forever, so the stress started to leak out in your sleep in the form of night terrors."

This was a revelation. I didn't have to fear the night terrors. In fact, I could trust them to alert me when I was overtaxed.

"So I just need to find a better way to deal with stress?"

"Exactly. That will work wonders. But it's also important to keep getting up and journaling every time you have a night terror. Doing that will retrain your mind. You're telling it that every time you have a terror, you're going to get out of bed and turn on a light and do some writing. This is going to cause you to lose even more sleep than if you had rolled over after the disturbance. You will be tired the next day, and your mind won't like that. Eventually, hopefully, if you pair this with better stress management, your mind will develop new ways of coping. Then you won't have so many night terrors."

This approach was a complete and total paradigm shift. The night terrors, the very thing that represented fear for me, were actually my body's way of helping me cope in life. It suddenly dawned on me what a marvel my body was. It had helped me survive and cope with unspeakable trauma at a ridiculously young age. And it was continuing to work hard to help me as an adult. Granted, its way of dealing with stress seemed a little outdated; there were better ways than night terrors to alert me to stress. But I had to give it points for trying. It had carried me all this way.

And the fact that I could retrain it to adopt new coping mechanisms? Worth its weight in gold, I tell ya. In fact, worthy of fireworks, parades (but no clowns), and an all-you-can-eat chocolate buffet complete with the world's best chocolate mousse. Because that meant I had some control over the situation. I was no longer passive, no longer a victim. I didn't have to be afraid anymore.

The second thing occurred around this same time. I was working with Lana, my fellow covenant group member, to plan a retreat for her church. For weeks we e-mailed back and forth to finalize the agenda and hammer out the details. One day my eyes scanned over her e-mail signature. At the bottom, below her name and contact info, I saw this: "Be at peace; you are deeply loved by God" (Dan. 10:19). I was unfamiliar with this verse, so I picked up a Bible and found the passage, though the wording differed. I decided to use my Bible app to flip through the translations. What I gleaned from the various versions was this: "Do not fear, for you are deeply loved by God. Be at peace."

I was speechless. *Do not fear.* I read this as God's confirmation that I no longer needed to be afraid. Why? Because I am deeply loved by God. Deeply. Loved. By God. In other words, God's got this. God was with my seven-year-old self during the trauma, and God was also present after the trauma as I tried to figure out how to cope. God had created me, giving me a body and mind that were capable of doing what needed to be done to foster my survival at the time. God had gotten me through decades of living in fear. And now, God was helping me see how I could retrain this miracle of a body to handle stress and fear. God was offering me new life—a life free from fear. A life full of peace.

This verse has come to represent my entire theology as well as my life and healing journey. I repeat it daily, sometimes multiple times a day, using this form: Do not fear. Deeply loved. Be at peace.

Because it has three short phrases, each with three syllables, it makes the perfect mantra, listening focus, and/or calming technique. It's great to use with prayer beads or as you go about your day. We do not have to be afraid because God is with us—ready to comfort us, sustain us, and carry us through the worst of times.

Let's be clear: I'm not saying that as soon as you read this your fears will be erased and life will be filled with rainbows and unicorns. As you've already figured out, it's not that easy. I believe you can reach a point where fear does not rule your life as it did mine for so long. As it may be ruling yours now. Finding some way to acknowledge your fears seems to be the first step. Then, learn what you can about them, identify what they are trying to tell you about yourself, and find other ways of coping. That way, you are in control.

Stacey once shared a fable about a woman who lived alone. Every day her Fears would come to visit. They would knock on the door, and she would let them in. Then they would spend the day being rude, causing havoc, swinging from the chandeliers, and staying long past their welcome. After a while, the woman had had all she could take. So the next time the Fears knocked on the door, the woman invited them in for tea and asked them to sit at the table. She announced that the Fears would be allowed to visit for a while, but then she would ask them to leave. And so it was. Together, they had tea at the table and talked, and when she was ready, the woman asked the Fears to leave. And they did, leaving the house as neat and tidy as when they first arrived.

This makes for a great parable, particularly when we can see Jesus in this story. Picture him standing with you as you acknowledge your Fears and invite them in. See him joining you as you sit with your Fears at the table, listening to what they have to teach you. Watch as he supports you in bidding them to leave when they are no longer useful. Experience the peace that comes as you realize that with the Fears' departure you are free to bask in Christ's presence and receive his grace.

I pray you will be able to trust the healing process. Though it may be slower than we like, God is there, guiding and comforting us along the way. Trust God. Trust God's *deep* love for you. Trust that you do not have to live in fear, believing that God has abandoned you. Indeed, God is with you, calling you to embrace a life of peace. That is the next chapter of your true story.

Reflection Questions

1. What role does fear play in your life? How does it affect you?
2. What are you afraid of? What forms does your fear take (for example, as nightmares, anxiety, controlling behaviors, etc.)?
3. What does it mean to you that healing is a process? Can you look back and see signs of the healing process at work in your life?
4. What does it mean to you to *trust* the process?
5. What difference will it make to you to acknowledge your fears?
6. What can you learn from your fears? from other emotions?
7. What difference does it make to know that God loves you deeply?

PRAYER BEAD EXPERIENCE

Cross: God of grace,

Invitatory bead: heal my spirit

Resurrection bead: by the power of your Son, Jesus Christ.

1ˢᵗ cruciform bead: Listen as I describe my fear.

Week beads, set 1: Use each bead to describe your fear to God—what it looks like, feels like, sounds like, and so on.

2ⁿᵈ cruciform bead: Hear me as I tell you what impact fear has had on me.

Week beads, set 2: Use each bead to share what fear has done to your life.

3ʳᵈ cruciform bead: Help me to acknowledge and learn from my fears.

Week beads, set 3: Use each bead to consider your fears and determine what you can learn from them.

4ᵗʰ cruciform bead: Heal me of my fear so I can experience your peace.

Week beads, set 4: Use each bead to pray for healing and to know that God loves you deeply and wants peace for you.

Resurrection bead: In the name of Jesus Christ,

Invitatory bead: who has the power to heal me.

Cross: Amen.

Listening Focus

Do not fear. Deeply loved. Be at peace.

What Do You Notice?

What insights, feelings, memories, or other wisdom arose as you read the chapter material or completed the prayer bead experience? Whom can you share this with?

Take a minute to use your prayer beads to connect with your body. Sit quietly and breathe deeply with each bead. As you do, stay present in the moment, releasing any concerns, anxiety, or distractions. Embrace this place of stillness with God before you continue in your journey.

EXPERIENCING GOD'S PEACE

All shall be well, and all shall be well,

and all manner of thing shall be well.

—Julian of Norwich

TRUST

Immediately Jesus made the disciples get into the boat and go on ahead of him to the other side, while he dismissed the crowd. After he had dismissed them, he went up on a mountainside by himself to pray. Later that night, he was there alone, and the boat was already a considerable distance from the land, buffeted by the waves because the wind was against it.

Shortly before dawn Jesus went out to them, walking on the lake. When the disciples saw him walking on the lake, they were terrified. "It's a ghost," they said, and cried out in fear.

But Jesus immediately said to them: "Take courage! It is I. Don't be afraid."

"Lord, if it's you," Peter replied, "tell me to come to you on the water."

"Come," he said.

Then Peter got down out of the boat, walked on the water and came toward Jesus. But when he saw the wind, he was afraid and, beginning to sink, cried out, "Lord, save me!"

Immediately Jesus reached out his hand and caught him. "You of little faith," he said, "why did you doubt?"

And when they climbed into the boat, the wind died down. Then those who were in the boat worshiped him, saying, "Truly you are the Son of God."

—MATTHEW 14:22-33

TRUTH-TELLING

To: My Academy Covenant Group Members
Sent: Wednesday, October 16, 2013 9:25:23 AM

Hey everyone—
I have continued to do a lot of good work and healing with my spiritual
director and therapist since we last met. If any of you read *The Shack* you
know that Mack, the main character whose daughter was kidnapped
and murdered, deals with The Great Sadness. At one point in the book
he talks with God about finally letting go of The Great Sadness and
seeing who he is without it.

I read this book again recently and realized I've carried The Great
Fear around all my life. But now I'm ready to release it so that I am free
to receive The Great Peace.

Both my therapist and spiritual director are encouraging me
to hold a "memorial service" to symbolically bury The Great Fear.
I've decided to do this during the next Academy session. It seems
perfect since Sumatanga is the place where I've experienced the most
profound healing. I know I want to go to Creel Chapel on the top of
the mountain at Sumatanga to do this. I don't know what day I'll do
this or what the service will look like, but it will be something simple.

Anyway, I wanted to invite all of you to join me.

Peace, Kristen

And so it was that I arrived for Academy session six ready to bury my fear.

The passage from *The Shack* had come at the right time: My perception
of the night terrors had shifted. I no longer asked my body to absorb the day's
turmoil so that its only recourse was a sleep disturbance. Instead, I was praying,
journaling, talking, and doing yoga to deal with stress. The night terrors had
decreased both in frequency and intensity. My husband commented one day
about a night disturbance I'd had the previous evening, but I had no memory
of anything happening. I called that a win. I had learned to trust the process,
and that had made all the difference. Fear no longer had a hold on me. In
fact, I could even acknowledge the ways in which it had helped me. Here is
a snippet from a journal entry on September 11, 2013:

At one time The Great Fear was a gift from God. It helped me cope—
alone—with an unimaginable trauma. And it kept me safe and helped

me survive other traumatic events as well. . . . I am so grateful for The Great Fear But now it's time to release it, to give it back to God and give thanks for how far I've come. Then I will be free to receive God's true gift for me: The Great Peace.

Not surprisingly, my covenant group members all responded immediately to my e-mail with messages of support and offers to help with the memorial service. I had never planned a memorial service before, but it seemed appropriate to use the healing service liturgy from *The Upper Room Worshipbook*; we used it during each Academy session, and it provided the perfect backdrop for burying something in order to receive God's peace. I assigned each of them a role in the service, though we waited until we had gathered at Camp Sumatanga to determine a day to hold it. In the end, we opted for Thursday, which just happened to be Halloween. Such an appropriate day to lay aside The Great Fear!

Before heading up the mountain I needed to do two things. First, I wrote my mom a letter. I knew this healing was as much for her as it was me. She had been a victim in all of this too. The bicycle guy's threats had denied her the opportunity to comfort me and help me heal, as well as to seek justice. And when, at the age of thirty-one, I finally told her about the molestation, she struggled with feelings of guilt, wondering how she had missed the signs (if there were any) or had failed to realize something traumatic had happened. She ached at the thought of my coping with the trauma at such a young age. Devastated, she sought the support of a therapist. Thus, I felt it important to write a letter and tell her I understood she was also a victim in all this and also needed God's healing grace. Writing the letter was my way of including her in the memorial service. I would be releasing The Great Fear for her as well.

Next, I went to Blake and told him about the service. "Ever since the night of my sermon I've felt a connection with you in my healing journey. And there's no pressure. I mean, I know you're busy, but I'd love it if you'd come to the service."

"I am so there!" He smiled. "You just tell me when and where."

"Great. And I'd love it if other members of the leadership team would join us, but I know they have a lot going on and may not be able to do that."

"You let me handle that. I'll see you at the service."

After lunch, my covenant group members and Paul, who by now was an integral part of my inner healing circle, loaded up in Lana's van and began the ten-minute journey up Chandler Mountain. Once there I began setting up the altar. I'd brought various items to represent my journey: a picture of me when I was seven, the picture of my mom and me at this very chapel, my "All shall be well" candle, a set of prayer beads, and an art print devoted to gratitude. Meanwhile, Amy searched for a place to dig a hole. The plan involved my burying seven rocks, each representing some aspect of The Great Fear. Amy had brought thirty-four "Easter" daffodil bulbs. In a symbolic gesture we were going to plant them over the buried rocks. Unfortunately, she couldn't find any place to dig in the solid ground.

"Guess I'll have to chuck them over the mountainside," I said. At that moment I looked up to see two cars arriving. As I watched, every member of the leadership team got out and headed over toward us. I was humbled and delighted. Each had played a significant role in my healing journey. I could not have asked for more. This was going to be perfect.

Janet led us through the liturgy, while Steve led us in singing "Amazing Grace." Nell read Psalm 91, then I read the passage from *The Shack* about Mack releasing The Great Sadness. Then I held up the first rock.

"When I was seven, I made a decision that changed my life. Ever since, I have feared making mistakes and failing. This rock represents that." I turned and threw the rock over the mountainside. "I now release that fear."

"This second rock represents my fear of being imperfect." I took a deep breath, turned, and lobbed it over the mountain. I did the same with rocks three (fear or rejection) and four (fear of giving up control).

The fifth rock choked me up. "This rock represents my fear of being hurt. I was hurt very badly when I was seven. I've been hurting ever since. But I don't need to carry this fear anymore. I am safe."

Picking up the sixth rock, I cried softly. "This rock is my fear of being killed, of being murdered." I took another deep breath, then threw it into the air with great force.

I picked up the last rock and considered it for a moment. "I spent much of my life believing that God had betrayed and abandoned me. Now I know that isn't true. This rock represents my fear of being abandoned and unloved by God." I turned and looked out over the valley. With every ounce of strength, I hurled the rock over the side of the cliff.

I turned back to see my friends smiling broadly.

Lana read the passage from Daniel, chapter 10. As she read verse 19, I looked around me. Here I was, standing on top of a mountain in this holy place on a gorgeous fall day. Better still, I was surrounded by people who had journeyed with me, listened to my truth, helped me recognize the image of God within me, sustained me in the dark times, and rejoiced with me as I healed. Along with them, in spirit, were my friends and family who had also journeyed with me. This group represented God's deep, gracious, and extravagant love for me. I was indeed at peace.

Steve ended the service by singing "It Is Well with My Soul." As he finished singing, he announced he had brought something to celebrate. And so it was that we marked God's grace in the most appropriate manner possible: with chocolate.

Later, during the quiet time, Amy and I went for a walk along the lake to find a place to plant the bulbs. We chose a place along the water, close to the outdoor labyrinth. As we dug in the dirt, I realized something. Looking up I said, "We're just below Creel Chapel. So, conceivably, the rocks I threw could have landed somewhere around here. But now, beautiful daffodils will be springing up in their place, and that's what people will see."

Amy smiled. "I think this was meant to be. Our plan to bury the rocks and then plant the bulbs up on the mountain was a good one, but I like this so much better. It was so powerful to see you throw the rocks over the mountain. It really affirmed that you were getting rid of those fears. And now, flowers will grow down here in this lovely place by the labyrinth."

She was right. It had been cathartic to hurl those seven rocks.

After reading a poem on healing, Amy left to finish her quiet time in solitude. I stayed by the lakeside and walked the labyrinth. Moving toward the center, I gave thanks to God for the healing God had wrought in my life and for the fact that I was able to release my fear and put it to rest. But my prayer changed once I reached the center. Having buried (or hurled) The Great Fear, the time had come to see what my life was like without it. It had defined me for most of my life and had become firmly ingrained in my identity. I acknowledged times when I had clung to it even as I prayed for the strength to let go of it. Now, I had done that. Who was I now? What would my life be like?

Surely this is how Peter feels as he watches Jesus beckon him to walk on water. He wants to do it; he is ready to trust Jesus but no doubt he is nervous too. What will happen when he steps out of the boat?

The unknown: that's what makes trust so difficult. We don't know what will happen—it could be good, but it could also be very, very bad, and as trauma survivors, we've seen the worst outcome of a situation. We've been burned and learned to play it safe for our own survival. But that's not sustainable. Life requires trust on a variety of levels and in myriad situations. And the larger issue is that God created us for relationship with God and one another, and trust is an integral part of living in relationship. Plus, trust can lead to joy, fullness, inspiration, wellness, and peace.

My friend Paul said "Trust the process." I would build on that to say trust *is* a process. It is a process of being vulnerable, taking risks, and determining which people, situations, and paths are safe. This means you can practice trust. It is like learning to swim: first, you dip your toe in the water to find that the water is warm and soft. Then you wade in and discover how good the water feels around you. You place your trust in someone as you lay on your back, supported at first by their hands, then gradually explore what it's like to float on your own. Soon, you are dipping your face below the water, learning to kick and propel yourself with your arms, venturing out into the deep end. And suddenly, you are swimming.

Thing is, it helps to want to swim. Sure, you can learn to swim even if you don't want to, though I'm guessing it may take longer and involve a lot of thrashing about. Likewise with trust in God or another person or even yourself: You may feel so betrayed that you no longer want to trust God. Then, over time, events may occur that lead you to realize you can trust again. But it's a tad easier when you want to trust and are willing to open yourself up even a little bit to recognize the ways in which God is there for you.

Exiting the labyrinth, I didn't know what to expect. And, yes, that was a bit scary but not in a Great Fear kind of way. I welcomed this kind of scary because it meant I was alive, fully present, and living into my calling.

It meant I was going to have to trust Jesus, myself, and those who supported me as I stepped out of the boat and onto the surface of the water.

It meant I was moving closer to peace.

REFLECTION QUESTIONS

1. Is there one particular feeling (sadness, fear, etc.) you struggle with?
2. Can you release the feelings you have struggled with? If so, how?
3. How could you mark the occasion of your releasing this weight?
4. What will life be like when you release this feeling? What will be different? How will you handle this?

5. Whom do you identify with in the story of Jesus walking on the water?
6. Do you trust God? Why or why not?
7. What do you need in order to build or deepen your trust in God?

Prayer Bead Experience

Cross: God of love,

Invitatory bead: help me to experience your peace

Resurrection bead: by the power of your Son, Jesus Christ.

1st cruciform bead: Lead me to a place of complete trust.

Week beads, set 1: Use each bead to open your heart to trust. Consider what that means for you.

2nd cruciform bead: Help me to trust you, dear Lord.

Week beads, set 2: Use each bead to consider how you can begin trusting God.

3rd cruciform bead: Help me to trust myself and others.

Week beads, set 3: Use each bead to consider how you can begin trusting yourself and others.

4th cruciform bead: Show me the difference trust will make in my life.

Week beads, set 4: Use each bead to contemplate the difference choosing trust will have in your life.

Resurrection bead: In the name of Jesus Christ,

Invitatory bead: who offers his peace.

Cross: Amen.

Listening Focus

Lord, I trust you.

What Do You Notice?

What insights, feelings, memories, or other wisdom arose as you read the chapter material or completed the prayer bead experience? Whom can you share this with?

Take a minute to use your prayer beads to connect with your body. Sit quietly and breathe deeply with each bead. As you do, stay present in the moment, releasing any concerns, anxiety, or distractions. Embrace this place of stillness with God before you continue your journey.

LOVE

Jesus answered, "Allow me to be baptized now. This is necessary to fulfill all righteousness."

So John agreed to baptize Jesus. When Jesus was baptized, he immediately came up out of the water. Heaven was opened to him, and he saw the Spirit of God coming down like a dove and resting on him. A voice from heaven said, "This is my Son whom I dearly love; I find happiness in him."

—MATTHEW 3:15-17

TRUTH-TELLING

For several years I had wanted to get a tattoo. Nothing big or flashy—just something small and simple on my wrist to represent my faith. I'm a visual person and thus am always drawn to visible signs and symbols. But granting that tattoos are, you know, permanent, I was in no hurry; I wanted to give myself plenty of time to find the right symbol, one that would hold a lifetime of meaning.

About halfway through The Academy, my friend Cyndi posted on Facebook that she wanted to get a tattoo on her wrist. A United Methodist pastor, she too wanted a faith symbol. I messaged her and told her we were on the same wavelength. We agreed to go together to get inked once we had each decided on a design. Cyndi said she wasn't sure yet but was considering a symbol around the word *hesed*. I had no clue what *hesed* meant but figured

I should know. It was probably some important concept we had covered in seminary that—like many things—I had just forgotten.

An internet search revealed that *hesed* is a Hebrew word used to describe the love God has for us and the love we are called to have for each other. Although *hesed* is most often translated as loving-kindness, scholars debate the exact translation; it's also been translated as mercy, loyalty, faithfulness, grace, goodness. The more I read, the more I realized this word captured (as much as any word can) the full attributes of God's love—a love that is kind, faithful, loyal, unfailing, unconditional, merciful, rich, wonderful, transformative, graceful, all-encompassing, exuberant, steadfast, and on and on. Whatever good quality you can come up with to describe God's love, *hesed* captures it. The word itself celebrates the love God has for us. And the one who embodied this love for us in every way is Jesus Christ.

Hesed shows up in many places throughout the Bible, but Psalm 23:6 caught my attention: "Surely goodness and mercy will follow me all the days of my life." The word *mercy* is *hesed* in the original translation. Thus, you can read this familiar prayer as, "Surely goodness and God's love will follow me all the days of my life." Good stuff. But it gets better. The word translated *follow* in the New Revised Standard Version actually means "pursue." So the psalmist reminds us that God's love is an active love, one that doesn't passively follow but actively pursues us all the days of our lives. How great is that?

Reading this verse, I knew instantly that I wanted a *hesed* tattoo. However, I hesitated because I didn't want to take Cyndi's idea and wasn't looking to get matching tattoos. I began considering other symbols. Then, one day, we chatted about our ideas for tattoos.

"What are you going to get?" she asked.

"I don't know," I said. "I was thinking of maybe having *imago dei* (image of God) written on my wrist, but it would be written twice: once facing me, and a second mirror image facing outward to the other person. So when I extend my hand to another person, the tattoo would remind both of us that we were created in God's image."

"No way!" Cyndi said. "I love that! The Genesis story and *imago dei* has always summarized my theology! I want that as my tattoo!"

I breathed a sigh of relief. "Perfect! Because I really want *hesed* for mine!"

And so it was that I had the Hebrew word *hesed* tattooed on my left wrist, with an arc of seven prayer beads above it. The prayer beads represent so much: the calling that led to my healing; the prayer tool that helps me to connect with God; the ministry that has brought innumerable, profound, testimonies of God's grace. I took the design for the prayer beads from my company logo, but I later realized the arc of the beads reminds me of the dimmer switch my friend Paul had talked about. I would forever have a symbol of God's deep love for me, which I came to understand through this healing process and miracle of a journey. I love my tattoo! It often surprises me and always makes me smile and give thanks.

Soon after, I decided I wanted to try a new prayer practice. I began saying the Jesus Prayer repeatedly at various times of the day. Christians have been reciting this prayer for over a thousand years. Because it's short, it makes a great breath prayer: a prayer you can say in connection with your breathing.

Inhale: Lord Jesus Christ, Son of God,

Exhale: have mercy on me, a sinner.

I practiced saying this prayer while folding laundry, walking the dog, driving to soccer practice. One day I sat at a red light while saying the prayer. Suddenly, I stopped on the second line: "have mercy on me." Mercy. My thoughts immediately returned to what I had recently learned about *hesed* and Psalm 23. What if I used *hesed* in the Jesus Prayer? Slowly, I prayed, "Lord Jesus Christ, Son of God, love me, a sinner." Though it didn't change the spirit of the prayer, the difference was profound. I was proclaiming God's love for me, connecting with it and inviting it into my heart. I couldn't believe it.

During session seven, Elaine Heath spoke passionately about the transformative power of God's love and how we are called to live out that love in tangible ways through community. In the plenary session one day, I shared my journey of learning about *hesed* and mercy and how that changed the way I prayed the Jesus Prayer.

"I'm not trying to be an iconoclast or anything. I believe praying as a sinner needing mercy is critical to remind us of our need for God's grace on a daily basis. But praying it this way has really been meaningful for me. It's helping me receive and own God's love for me," I said.

"That's profound," Elaine responded. "I can't wait to hear how it sounds when you finish it."

Finish it? I thought I *was* finished with it.

I pondered the prayer, going over each word carefully. I knew I didn't want to change anything in the first line; I relished the chance to proclaim Jesus as Lord and Son of God. That left the last part of the second line: "... a sinner." I considered that for a moment. What would it mean to change that? And what would I change it to?

My mind instantly returned to session six when Sister Kathleen spoke about Jesus and the woman with the hemorrhage. He had called her "daughter." I envisioned myself standing before Jesus, asking him to love me, knowing he would call me daughter too. Indeed, I heard him call me "beloved daughter." Elaine was right; I had needed to finish revising this prayer.

Inhale: Lord Jesus Christ, Son of God,

Exhale: love me, your beloved daughter.

That was it. That was my Jesus Prayer. Suddenly, this short ancient prayer became deeply personal for me, professing my faith in God's healing *hesed* and hearing God's gentle response. I realized I had come to own God's deep, unending, faithful, passionate, glorious love for me. In giving up The Great Fear, I had created space for The Great Love. I have become so convinced of God's *hesed* that I find myself referring to "God's deep love" at every turn. No doubt you have seen this phrase multiple times throughout the book.

Life of the Beloved by Henri Nouwen is, in essence, a love letter written for Fred, a close friend of Nouwen's. Fred, a Jew, asked Nouwen to write a book on spirituality for him and his friends, many of whom did not identify as religious. He wanted thoughts on spirituality, thoughts about God that his friends could hear and understand. As Nouwen considered Fred's request, he realized many others around him had a similar yearning for a book that would speak to their deepest needs and desire for God. Nouwen, familiar with writing for a Christian audience, found himself challenged to come up with what to say. But he sat in the stillness and listened to the needs of Fred and those like him, which led him to one word: *Beloved*.

One primary place we hear this word is in the story of Jesus' baptism. As Jesus rises out of the water of the Jordan River, the Holy Spirit, in the form of a dove, descends from heaven. At the same time, a voice from heaven breaks forth and declares, "This is my Son whom I dearly love." In a number of other translations, this reads, "You are my Son, the Beloved."

I have always valued this scene. We're seeing Jesus as an adult for the first time. Last time we saw him he was twelve and giving his parents a panic attack after wandering away from them into the Temple. We have no idea what he's been up to since then, but here we see him ready to begin his ministry. He marks the occasion by having his cousin, John, baptize him in the Jordan River along with everyone else who has come to be baptized that day. In a sense, Jesus is just one of us. And yet, he's not. There's something special about this guy because when he rises out of the water, heaven opens up, the Holy Spirit descends, and we hear a voice from heaven, which I assume is God's voice. We realize Jesus is both divine and human. Jesus is God's "beloved." God claims Jesus in a relationship that is founded in a deep, extraordinary love.

This makes sense. Of course Jesus is God's beloved. But, as Nouwen suggests, so are we. We who have been formed out of dust and breathed into life so that we can be in relationship with God: We are God's beloved. We who have been created *imago dei*: We are God's beloved. We who have been pursued to the ends of the earth by God's *hesed*: We are God's beloved. We who were joined on earth by Jesus—God in human flesh—so that we might know God intimately: We are God's beloved. We who stood at the foot of the cross and watched as Jesus died so that we would have eternal life: We are God's beloved. We who were surprised by the joy of an empty tomb on Easter morning: We are God's beloved. We who continue to grow in and out of faith, living as best we can in a world we don't understand and that often fails us: We are God's beloved.

The world finds it surprising to learn that it is God's beloved; this is particularly true for those of us who have survived trauma. For all the reasons we have named in this book, particularly the feelings of grief, anger, abandonment, fear, and shame, we have doubted our belovedness. Many of us have lost sight of it entirely, believing there's no way God's beloved would have to endure what we've been through. But that is when we have to remember we do not allow our condition to define us. We did not experience trauma because we lay beyond God's love, nor does our trauma cancel out our belovedness. One of my favorite passages from Nouwen's book is this: "Self-rejection is the greatest enemy of the spiritual life because it contradicts the sacred voice that calls us the 'Beloved.' Being the Beloved expresses the core truth of our existence" (p. 33). Surviving a trauma is one thing that happened to you; it is not the core truth of your existence. Beloved is who you are, who you have always been, and who you will always be.

Go, and be loved.

REFLECTION QUESTIONS

1. What words would you use to describe God's love?
2. What does it mean to you that God's love pursues you?
3. What does it mean to you that God loves you deeply? Do you believe that?
4. What are the ways in which you have experienced God's love for you? When have you not felt it?
5. How has the trauma changed the way you feel about God's love for you?
6. What does it mean to you that you are God's beloved? How does that impact your self-identity?
7. Do you believe Nouwen's statement that "being the Beloved expresses the core truth" of your existence? Why or why not?

PRAYER BEAD EXPERIENCE

Cross: God of love,

Invitatory bead: help me to experience your peace

Resurrection bead: by the power of your Son, Jesus Christ.

1st cruciform bead: For so long, I have not felt beloved.

Week beads, set 1: Use each bead to express the ways in which you have not felt God's love for you.

2nd cruciform bead: I need to be reminded of your love, dear Lord.

Week beads, set 2: Use each bead to listen for God's voice of deep love in your life. What does it sound like? What do you hear?

3rd cruciform bead: Help me to reclaim my belovedness.

Week beads, set 3: Use each bead to listen for and reconnect with the part of you that knows you are beloved.

4th cruciform bead: Guide me to live as your beloved.

Week beads, set 4: Use each bead to consider what it will be like to live as God's beloved. What will that look like? What will be different?

Resurrection bead: In the name of Jesus Christ,

Invitatory bead: who offers his peace.

Cross: Amen.

Listening Focus

I am God's beloved.

What Do You Notice?

What insights, feelings, memories, or other wisdom arose as you read the chapter material or completed the prayer bead experience? Whom can you share this with?

Take a minute to use your prayer beads to connect with your body. Sit quietly and breathe deeply with each bead. As you do, stay present in the moment, releasing any concerns, anxiety, or distractions. Embrace this place of stillness with God before you continue in your journey.

FORGIVENESS

After a few days, Jesus went back to Capernaum, and people heard that he was at home. So many gathered that there was no longer space, not even near the door. Jesus was speaking the word to them. Some people arrived, and four of them were bringing to him a man who was paralyzed. They couldn't carry him through the crowd, so they tore off part of the roof above where Jesus was. When they had made an opening, they lowered the mat on which the paralyzed man was lying. When Jesus saw their faith, he said to the paralytic, "Child, your sins are forgiven!"

Some legal experts were sitting there, muttering among themselves, "Why does he speak this way? He's insulting God. Only the one God can forgive sins."

Jesus immediately recognized what they were discussing, and he said to them, "Why do you fill your minds with these questions? Which is easier—to say to a paralyzed person, 'Your sins are forgiven,' or to say, 'Get up, take up your bed, and walk'? But so you will know that the Human One has authority on the earth to forgive sins," he said to the man who was paralyzed, "Get up, take your mat, and go home."

Jesus raised him up, and right away he picked up his mat and walked out in front of everybody. They were all amazed and praised God, saying, "We've never seen anything like this!"

—MARK 2:1-12

Truth-Telling

I confess that I've never spent a lot of time wondering whether to forgive the bicycle guy. The trauma occurred so long ago and I had hidden it so well that I couldn't muster up enough anger at him. Fear was my prevalent emotion. Plus, I couldn't remember his face, didn't know his name, and knew I would never see him again, so I didn't get really worked up about him personally. From time to time I would think about forgiveness. I conceded that I should forgive him, but I didn't understand how to go about it. So, I focused on other aspects of life.

That's all to say, I wasn't seeking forgiveness when I signed up for a reiki session.

Oops. Wait a minute. Don't go anywhere. I know the idea of a reiki session may sound flaky or non-Christian or just plain weird to some of you. I get it. But hear me out.

The reiki idea first came about after watching a TV show in which an adult woman was trying to access memories about childhood abuse. After years of therapy, she still couldn't access some of the memories, so someone encouraged her to try reiki, an alternative form of stress reduction and healing. Practitioners "lay hands" on the person (though generally their hands hover over, rather than actually touch, the person's body) to harness the person's "energy." The idea is that when we suffer trauma, our bodies hold the physical memories and responses to the trauma, so reiki provides a way of helping the body release that. Following the show, I heard a few other people talk about reiki and its use in relation to trauma. I was curious. The night terrors were still a way of life, though by now they had dissipated in frequency and impact and were inspiring me to learn new ways to manage my stress. Still, I had to confess that they signaled that my body was holding on to the trauma. I wanted to help release it.

In sharing this idea with my therapist and yoga teacher, both recommended a woman named Eva. I trusted their judgment and called to book an appointment. On the given day, I spent some time talking with Eva and sharing some of my story. Then I lay fully clothed on the massage table while she hovered her hands over me, moving them back and forth over my body. Periodically, she would talk about my "chakras" or "energy," but for the most part she worked silently. Eyes closed, I relaxed, prayed, and rested.

About thirty minutes into the hour-long session, Eva was holding her hands over my stomach when a vision popped into my mind. I saw my seven-year-old self standing on the sidewalk. Across from me was the bicycle guy. It was the moment when he approached me and had begun talking with me. In that moment, a group of beings floated down from the sky and in between us. If you've ever read *The Shack*, you will recall the scene where Mack sees his father with a large group of people in heaven. Mack describes his father and the others as beings of light—ethereal and floaty. That's what these beings looked like in my vision.

As they came between us, I thought, *Oh, they're going to come between us to protect me.* Except they didn't stop. Instead, they flew around me until they surrounded me, completely encircling me in love and protection. In unison, they said, "We love you and want good things for you. And we don't want you to do this because it's not good for you."

They didn't want me to walk away with the bicycle guy.

Almost immediately, another group of light beings flew down from the sky and between us. Again I thought, *Okay, this group is going to stand between us and block him.* But they continued their graceful flight until they had encircled the bicycle guy. "We love you and want good things for you. And we don't want you to do this because it's not good for you."

I was stunned. The floaty light beings wanted good things not just for me but for the bicycle guy as well. They loved and wanted to protect him too.

"I think I just forgave the molester," I said.

"No way! Really?" said Eva.

I described what I'd just seen.

"That gives me chills," she said.

Me too. For the next several days I felt a lightness I had never experienced before. It wasn't so much that I had carried a heavy burden and now felt released from it. It was more that I saw the world in a whole new way. I realized I had been given the gift of seeing other people as God sees them: with deep love. I understood that God loves every person on this planet and has created them for good purposes. I also came clear on the fact that when humans choose to go against those good purposes, it's because of our choices rather than because of God's plan, will, or actions. I had always *known* that, but now I understood it. I *felt* it.

Seeing the bicycle guy as God did made it easy and natural to forgive him. I could see that he was God's creation, someone whom God loved deeply. I could also see his brokenness that had led to his decision to assault me. God hadn't wanted that to happen. Moreover, God wanted the opportunity to redeem the bicycle guy, to heal his brokenness and return him to a state of goodness. Knowing God had the power to do that, I could release the guy to God with a heart full of light and love.

Forgiveness is hard, especially if you have experienced intentional harm. You may have no desire to forgive at all, preferring to imagine the person rotting in prison or in your own private, highly detailed version of the afterlife for him or her. In other cases, the desire may exist, but you may not know how to go about it. It can feel impossible.

I expect that's what we see in our scripture passage here. A man who is paralyzed has friends who bring him to Jesus for healing. As they draw close, they realize they cannot reach Jesus, who is surrounded by a great crowd. Undeterred, they consider their options, ultimately choosing to climb to the roof, tear a hole in it, and lower their friend down to Jesus.

What happens next, however, is both fascinating and confusing. Jesus sees the faith of the man's friends and declares that the man's sins are forgiven. Doesn't that seem strange? I mean, the man is brought there for healing from paralysis not for the forgiveness of his sins. Is Jesus having an off day? Is he not paying attention? Or is something else going on?

My husband, Max, helped me understand this passage. Max is a brilliant preacher, known for his ability to present God's word in an accessible, insightful, and often funny way. But on January 24, 2016—Max's birthday— he preached a sermon that will go down in history as one of his all-time best. (You will find the link to the video in Resources.) In it, Max told the story of his older brother, John, who was murdered in 2004. Using this scripture as the foundation, he spoke about the difficulty of forgiving the man convicted of the murder. I remember this time in our lives well. I remember watching Max as he struggled through this process. It was gut-wrenching. How do you forgive someone who deliberately and violently cuts a life short, robbing you of a beloved family member? It felt impossible.

That's what Jesus is saying: We cannot offer true forgiveness; it's not possible. We weren't built for that. On a good day, we humans have limitations in offering forgiveness; on a bad day, especially when a trauma has occurred, we can't do it at all. We cannot see beyond our own pain. We would be better off trying to work miracles of healing. Which is harder—telling someone to pick up their mat and walk, or telling them their sins are forgiven? From a human perspective, both are impossible.

But the good news is that Jesus, the One who makes all things new, has the power to offer forgiveness. That's the first thing this story tells us. Through faith, we can participate in this restoration. We bring our wounds to God, point to the ones who have caused us pain, and after screaming and asking for their heads on a platter, we ask for help in forgiving them. That was the most—and the best—that Max could do. It was the only possible option.

The other is this: The passage notes that Jesus saw the faith of the man's friends, which makes me wonder about the man's faith. Perhaps the man does not have enough faith at the time his friends lower him through the roof. He may have had none at all; the story doesn't tell us. But that doesn't matter. Jesus sees that the man's friends have faith and that seems to be enough.

I don't know about you, but I'm so relieved by this!

Like in the song "Lean on Me," at times we must rely on the faith of those around us. Have you ever felt like you couldn't pray? Despair, fatigue, anger, or confusion may have overwhelmed you, and you couldn't bring yourself to share your heart with God. Have there been times when you felt like you didn't believe in God? Or in the church? When you didn't feel worthy of God's love, healing, or forgiveness? We all have those moments when our faith feels broken and God seems too far away. That's okay. God's grace is so vast that it works even when our faith doesn't. God's grace is at work through the ones whose faith *is* working—the faith of our family members, our friends, our church members, our coworkers, and even strangers who pray for us when we don't even realize it.

I believe the vision I had during the reiki session with Eva resulted from people lifting me in prayer. Whether I knew it or not, their prayers were carrying me in the moments when I could not carry myself, until finally I could see the bicycle guy as Jesus sees him and participate in an act that was always above my pay grade.

This experience has changed the way I view the world. I see people in a whole new light. I see them as God sees them, with light and love and the best of intentions, with brokenness and a deep need for redemption. I see myself this way too. God's mercy is vast, and I am invited to be a part of it. So are you.

What a gift of grace.

Reflection Questions

1. Why is it necessary to forgive? What difference can forgiveness make in your life?
2. Whom do you need to forgive?
3. What makes it hard to offer forgiveness?
4. What would it look like to see the people you need to forgive as God sees them? What difference would this make?
5. How can we participate in the forgiveness that God offers?
6. When has your faith wavered or you felt lost? What was happening in your life at the time?
7. What does it mean to you to know that you can rely on the faith of others?

Prayer Bead Experience

Cross: God of love,

Invitatory bead: help me to experience your peace

Resurrection bead: by the power of your Son, Jesus Christ.

1st cruciform bead: I need to offer forgiveness.

Week beads, set 1: Use each bead to confess your need to forgive. Consider why forgiveness is important in your healing journey.

2nd cruciform bead: It feels impossible to offer forgiveness.

Week beads, set 2: Use each bead to acknowledge the difficulty you face in offering forgiveness.

3rd cruciform bead: Help me to participate in the forgiveness you offer.

Week beads, set 3: Use each bead to ask God to forgive the person or people you need to forgive.

4th cruciform bead: Help me to see others as you see them.

Week beads, set 4: Use each bead to watch how God sees other people.

Resurrection bead: In the name of Jesus Christ,

Invitatory bead: who offers his peace.

Cross: Amen.

Listening Focus

Jesus has the power to forgive.

What Do You Notice?

What insights, feelings, memories, or other wisdom arose as you read the chapter material or completed the prayer bead experience? Whom can you share this with?

Take a minute to use your prayer beads to connect with your body. Sit quietly and breathe deeply with each bead. As you do, stay present in the moment, releasing any concerns, anxiety, or distractions. Embrace this place of stillness with God before you continue in your journey.

GRATITUDE

On the way to Jerusalem, Jesus traveled along the border between Samaria and Galilee. As he entered a village, ten men with skin diseases approached him. Keeping their distance from him, they raised their voices and said, "Jesus, Master, show us mercy!"

When Jesus saw them, he said, "Go, show yourselves to the priests." As they left, they were cleansed. One of them, when he saw that he had been healed, returned and praised God with a loud voice. He fell on his face at Jesus' feet and thanked him. He was a Samaritan. Jesus replied, "Weren't ten cleansed? Where are the other nine? No one returned to praise God except this foreigner?" Then Jesus said to him, "Get up and go. Your faith has healed you."

—LUKE 17:11-19

TRUTH-TELLING

I am not a morning person. I'm just not, especially when it requires getting up early. And by early I mean before ten. But The Academy leadership did not see fit to adjust the daily schedule to my needs, and so it was that I got up, showered, and showed up for morning prayer at 7:30 a.m. every day.

Though painful, I admit that I learned to love this part of our day. The Great Silence, which we had observed since the conclusion of the previous day's night prayer, was broken only by the liturgy of morning prayer. As such, the retreat center was quiet when we arrived to find our seats. Kathy and Pat, members of the leadership team, always greeted us warmly, albeit silently, with a smile and a hug as they ushered us into the worship space. Waiting for the others to arrive (though I was usually among the last to get there), folks would pray or knit or look around. The silence created a space for reverence, listening, being still, taking deep breaths. For me, at least, it was always hopeful, an opportunity to anticipate the day and all it would hold for us.

Finally, Irene would ding the bell, and together we would stand and begin the day with this prayer:

> New every morning is your love, great God of light, and all day long you are working for good in the world. Stir up in us a desire to serve you, to live peacefully with our neighbors and all your creation, and to devote each day to your Son, our Savior Jesus Christ. Amen.
> —From "A Liturgy for Morning Prayer," *Upper Room Worshipbook*

Praying this prayer every morning, the words managed to seep into my soul, to the point that I continue to say them to this day (though generally at the more reasonable hours of nine or ten). What I love is that the prayer proclaims God as a God of love who offers that love fresh each day. We need not hold over from the previous day any grudges, sins, or regrets—God's love can wipe them away. We get a fresh start with God, whose love is more abundant than our hearts can fathom. Even better: God's purposes are good. God always works toward "good in the world," again, because God is about love. And we are invited to participate in that good by serving God, enjoying peaceful community with everyone and creation, and devoting our lives to Jesus. We proclaim that the day is based in love and goodness. We acknowledge this truth. It is, in essence, a prayer of deep gratitude.

This prayer has it roots in Lamentations 3:23, which talks about God's faithful love and compassion being "renewed every morning." And this passage lies at the heart of a particular Jewish tradition. Customarily Jews wake in the morning and before rolling out of bed or doing anything else, say, "Modeh ani" or ("Modah ani" for us womenfolk), which is Hebrew for "I am grateful." Like the Academy prayer, this tradition sets the tone for the day.

I had never practiced expressing gratitude on a regular basis. I am awful at writing thank-you notes, despite my mom's and grandmother's best efforts to instill this habit in me. And I tried to keep a gratitude journal, but it met the same fate as all my other journals. But somehow, waking up and saying *modah ani* and reciting the Academy morning prayer became a gratitude practice I could maintain. That was my first surprise.

The second came in the difference this small change made in my life. I began to notice things for which to be grateful: a cool summer breeze,

Max cooking dinner, my son's laughter, a good book to read. Small things, yes, but they helped me stay present in the moment. Instead of worrying about a comment someone made at church or whether we were going to have enough cake at my son's party on Saturday, I could focus on what was happening in my life at the moment and see God's presence in it. This served as another reminder that God is always with me; I just have to be willing to pay attention and see the signs of God's presence. The more I practiced gratitude, the more in touch I felt with God. I was convinced of God's presence, convinced of God's goodness, convinced of God's abundant love. This proved true even in difficult times, when perhaps the only thing I could find to appreciate at the moment was that the sun had risen or I had shoes to wear or I could taste the butter on a warm slice of bread. I could now find God in the darkness, and I felt exceedingly grateful. I began to understand how important gratitude was to my healing.

In the Luke story, Jesus encounters ten lepers who beg to be healed. Instead of healing them instantly, Jesus instructs the men to go show themselves to the priests. As lepers, they are outcasts from society; in order to return to their families and communities, they need to be declared "clean" by the priests. This act requires faith on the part of the men; they still have the disease as they obediently turn and do as Jesus commands. Only in the act of going forward in faith do they actually receive cleansing. Possibly, they do not realize it at first, until, step by step, they feel better; they notice that their skin clears, and their eyesight improves. They have been healed. Eventually, all ten arrive at the Temple free of their disease and, presumably, the priests declare them fit to return to society.

I can imagine that scene. The men, many of whom have been outcasts for years or even decades, must have been full of joy to be illness-free and able to return to their lives. I'm sure they immediately ran home to reunite with their wives, children, parents, and other loved ones. There were hugs, tears, shouts of "My, look how you've grown!" And stories of this Jesus who has shown them mercy.

But only one of them returns to offer thanks to Jesus. The Bible tells us nothing more about this particular man, nor do we know why the other nine do not return with him. Perhaps they are so overcome by the change in their condition that they hurry to attend to all the activities they could not participate in previously. They may have had every intention of expressing their gratitude but couldn't find the perfect notecard to send or else waited too long and then worried it was too late to offer thanks (she said, speaking from experience). Or they may have simply taken their healing for granted, believing it Jesus' job to work a miracle in their lives.

Too bad, because it appears that expressing gratitude is a critical step toward wholeness. You can tell by the changed dynamic between the man and Jesus. Whereas before the ten lepers had to keep their distance from Jesus, this man falls prostrate at Jesus' feet. There is no longer space between them. And whereas the ten lepers lamented their disease, begging Jesus for a cure, this man now finds himself free to "praise God with a loud voice." Sure, the healing has allowed for this coming together but so has the man's decision to return to Jesus. He has taken a significant step in his healing, one that helps him recognize he is not alone—that a relationship of faith is central to the process. When he faces future trials and heartaches (and they will come), he will know from experience that cries for mercy can lead to shouts of thankfulness.

Jesus acknowledges this truth by declaring, "Your faith has healed you!" In this instance, the word for "healed" differs from the word used in verse 15 (when the man "saw that he had been healed"). Here, Jesus does not speak about physical cure but spiritual wholeness. There is a difference. Cure focuses on the physical body, while wholeness involves the whole person: body, heart, mind, and soul. In returning to express gratitude, the man has come full circle in his healing journey, from begging for mercy to moving forward in faith to experiencing improvements to offering gratitude. In her book, *Searching for Sunday,* Rachel Held Evans writes, "I can't begin to heal until I've acknowledged my pain" (p. 222). Perhaps we can't be whole until we've acknowledged the Healer.

As I mentioned earlier, Brené Brown describes how shame destroys connection. We noted that trauma survivors who feel shame may become disconnected from God, others, and themselves. Brown spends a great deal of time explaining how shame resilience—the process of kicking shame to the curb—involves protecting and/or reestablishing connection. She argues that one primary way that people who feel shame try to shield themselves is through "foreboding joy." That is, they don't trust it when life is going well. They are so used to being hurt or disappointed that joy feels too risky. As soon as things seem to be going well, they immediately begin to watch for the other shoe to drop, believing, as they do, that they are not worthy of joy. She writes, "In a culture of deep scarcity—of never feeling safe, certain, and sure enough—joy can feel like a setup" (p. 118). I feel this is an important point in our discussion of healing. Often we spend so much time feeling lost, afraid, and victimized that it becomes our way of life, one we don't question. We perceive happiness as a temporary state until we return to drabness, which feels normal.

But God did not create a drab world; God created a world of wonder and mystery for us to experience, explore, and enjoy. God is working a process of healing in our lives so that we may return to a place of joy. We were meant for joy so we must practice gratitude, which, as Brown writes, is "the antidote to foreboding joy." Offering gratitude helps us reconnect and stay connected to God, others, and ourselves. It calls us to awareness and presence, allowing us to see the fullness of our lives no matter the circumstances. It soothes our grief, anger, sense of abandonment, shame, and fear, and feeds our trust, love, and desire for forgiveness and wholeness. The practice of gratitude reminds us that, as Julian of Norwich once said, "All shall be well, and all shall be well, and all manner of thing shall be well."

The most stunning example of gratitude came to me in a book written by Etty Hillesum. Etty, a young Jewish writer during World War II, lived just down the street from Anne Frank in Amsterdam. Like Anne's diary, Etty's journal entries collected in *An Interrupted Life* and *Letters from Westerbork* offer a glimpse of life in Amsterdam during this period. Etty describes how the Nazis increasingly controlled the daily lives of local Jews until they began to ship them off to Westerbork and other transit camps where they were held until being sent to the extermination camps. Etty's story stands out, however, because of her deep faith.

Etty, clearly well respected in her community, moved among influential circles, which afforded her many opportunities to hide from the Germans or leave the country. But Etty declined these offers. She wanted to go to the camp. She *wanted* to be sent to a concentration camp. Can you imagine?

Etty explained her decision in this way: "It still all comes down to the same thing: life is beautiful. And I believe in God. And I want to be there right in the thick of what people call 'horror' and still be able to say: life is beautiful" (p. 226). Etty recognized the extent of the suffering in the camps. She knew people would give up hope and possibly even their faith in God. Etty wanted to be with these people and bear witness to God's comforting presence. As she wrote, "We should be willing to act as a balm for all wounds" (p. 231). So Etty and her family were shipped off to Westerbork, and her faith remained strong. I find it extraordinary that her faith in a just and loving God never wavered.

For almost a year, Etty stayed busy ministering to people in Westerbork. All the while, she wrote in her journal. About a week before she and her family would be sent to their deaths in Auschwitz, Etty wrote the following:

> My life has become an uninterrupted dialogue with You, oh God, one great dialogue. Sometimes when I stand in some corner of the camp, my feet planted on Your earth, my eyes raised toward Your heaven, tears sometimes run down my face, tears of deep emotion and gratitude (p. 332).

I find this to be one of the most profound passages I have ever read. Surrounded by the darkest pain, the most visible signs of suffering and evil, and the knowledge of her impending death, Etty stands in the midst and proclaims her gratitude for God's rich beauty. Her life has become "an uninterrupted dialogue" with God; her entire life has become a prayer.

There are many good reasons for cultivating a life of gratitude, but I believe this reveals the most critical: There is pain in our world, and life is not always easy. As many of us have seen, at times it is downright traumatic and we feel we cannot take another breath. By practicing gratitude, we remember God's presence with us in the darkness as well as the light. We do not have to endure anything alone. Better still, we gain assurance that God helps us get through the darkness, shares our pain, ministers to us, and leads us toward peace. God is doing this as surely as God is offering God's love anew to us each day, stirring up in us a desire to serve God, live peacefully, and devote each day to God's Son, our Savior Jesus Christ.

REFLECTION QUESTIONS

1. What difference might gratitude make in your life?
2. How do you understand the story of the ten lepers?
3. Do you believe that God created you for joy? Why or why not?
4. What do you think about Etty Hillesum's quotes?
5. How is it possible to practice gratitude even in the face of tragedy?
6. Do you practice gratitude in your life? If so, what does it look like?
7. How can you develop a practice of gratitude?

PRAYER BEAD EXPERIENCE

Cross: God of love,

Invitatory bead: help me to experience your peace

Resurrection bead: by the power of your Son, Jesus Christ.

1st cruciform bead: Lord, I confess that sometimes it's difficult to offer gratitude.

Week beads, set 1: Use each bead to acknowledge the ways in which you struggle with gratitude.

2nd cruciform bead: Yet I acknowledge the difference gratitude can make in my life.

Week beads, set 2: Use each bead to consider the ways in which gratitude can impact your life.

3rd cruciform bead: Help me to recognize the ways in which you are present in my life and to offer my gratitude.

Week beads, set 3: Use each bead to practice awareness of God's presence and the gifts for which you are grateful.

4th cruciform bead: In particular, help me to recognize your presence in the darkness.

Week beads, set 4: Use each bead to pray for knowledge of God's presence in tough times.

Resurrection bead: In the name of Jesus Christ,

Invitatory bead: who offers his peace.

Cross: Amen.

Listening Focus

I am grateful.

What Do You Notice?

What insights, feelings, memories, or other wisdom arose as you read the chapter material or completed the prayer bead experience? Whom can you share this with?

Take a minute to use your prayer beads to connect with your body. Sit quietly and breathe deeply with each bead. As you do, stay present in the moment, releasing any concerns, anxiety, or distractions. Embrace this place of stillness with God before you continue in your journey.

PEACE

"I have spoken these things to you while I am with you. The Companion, the Holy Spirit, whom the Father will send in my name, will teach you everything and will remind you of everything I told you.

"Peace I leave with you. My peace I give you. I give to you not as the world gives. Don't be troubled or afraid."

—JOHN 14:25-27

TRUTH-TELLING

The following are among my favorite memories of the final session, session eight, of The Academy.

Robert Benson, one of my favorite writers, stood before us every afternoon to talk about a Rule of Life and how we can use it to sustain us in our Christian life. We were going to be leaving The Academy and needed to be able to take all we had learned with us into the world. He reminded us that God had created each of us uniquely, infusing us with particular gifts that were essential in creating God's kingdom dream. Rather than comparing ourselves to others or feeling that our gifts are of no consequence, Robert urged us to use the talents with which God has entrusted us. Only then will we bring God's dream to completion in all its glory. "Be who God called you to be," he said. "Be Kristen."

In the mornings we heard from Dale Clem, the other faculty for this session. He was charged with describing how we could go into the world and bear witness to the reign of God. No small task. He began by sharing his story of trauma. We knew pieces of the story since his wife, Kelly, participated in this Academy with us. Kelly pastored Goshen United Methodist Church in Piedmont, Alabama, when a tornado swept through town during church services on Palm Sunday, 1994. Among the twenty killed in the church was their four-year-old daughter, Hannah. In the aftermath, Dale and Kelly sought comfort in God, confident that God understood their suffering since God had also lost a child. To the surprise of many, they "dared to stand in the midst of death and destruction and speak of a loving God" (p. 46). Dale's book *Winds of Fury, Circles of Grace* offers a significant witness to God's reign by celebrating God's presence and goodness in the midst of tragedy.

Tables full of notebooks, photos, and trifold cardboard displays like the ones I used in high school science fairs lined the retreat center's hallway. These represented our final Academy projects. In the second year of the Academy we were charged with creating a project that represented something we wanted to do in the world as a result of our time in the Academy. There were Bible studies and offerings of Five-Day Academies in people's home states. One person developed Picture Book Theology, a blog and curriculum for using secular children's picture books to illustrate biblical themes and promote Sunday school discussions. Several developed projects related to prayer beads, their history, and their use in ministry. My project was the proposal that led to this book. All the projects reflected the myriad ways God was working in our lives and calling us to minister to the world.

Sitting in our conference room, lit by a single lamp and the Christ candle, my covenant group members and I gathered in a circle. On the table in the center sat a bag of Almond Joys—our signature snack. As we munched, we shared what we had learned and experienced in our two-year journey and dreamed about where God might lead us next. We promised to stay in touch and made plans to reunite in New Orleans that October. In reality, it would be October 2015—seventeen months later and back at Camp Sumatanga—before I would see the faces of my most-beloved friends again. Of all the folks in the Academy, these were the ones who knew me best. They listened to me, challenged me, laughed with me, prayed for me, and dreamed God's dreams with me. When I sit now and reflect on my time at Sumatanga, these are the faces that greet me first.

Walking back from night prayer each evening, traveling along the path toward my room, The Great Silence was broken only by the hoots of a nearby owl. Its long trills were expansive, filling the darkness with a haunting, melodic call that enveloped me in the stillness. I found it gorgeous, soothing, mystical.

My favorite memory, however, came on the evening of Friday, May 9, 2014, at our commissioning. Following a splendid meal for which we had gotten all dressed up, we filed into the worship space. In the center of the room were kneeling rails arranged in a semicircle, and we took turns coming up to the rails by covenant groups to be prayed over. One by one, Johnny placed a solid bronze cross in our hand while the leaders laid hands on us. As they did, Pat prayed, "May God's power work in you to do infinitely more than you can ask or imagine." Over and over, person by person, Pat repeated this prayer. Forty-three people made up our graduating class; forty-three times we heard those words: "May God's power work in you to do infinitely more than you can ask or imagine." After two years, eight sessions, forty days, sixty hours in covenant groups, eighty presentations, one hundred twenty worship services, countless hours spent in community, and even more in silence and solitude, we were being commissioned to go into the world fueled by God's power. It was a call to trust in God and in God's power to work through us to produce more than we could "ask or imagine." It was a call to be Kristen or Sally or Randy or Dan. It was a call to bear witness to God's goodness and mercy.

The next morning we gathered for Morning Prayer, then breakfast, then the final faculty sessions. Lastly, we gathered one last time in the worship space for the service of the Eucharist. As we prayed the liturgy and listened to the homily, I could feel tears welling up. It was an emotional time for all of us. As I prayed the words of The Great Thanksgiving, the feelings continued to rise so that by the time I got up to receive the elements, I was openly weeping. I knelt at one of the rails and sank into my emotions, crying as hard as I had at the foot of the wailing wall. Yet these were not tears of anguish and deep pain. Instead, they were a mixture of profound gratitude for my healing journey, deep relief at reaching a place of peace rather than fear in my life, and sadness over the end of my Academy experience. I knew this mountaintop experience could never be replicated. To be sure, I would participate in other amazing, wonderful, sacred experiences in my life; but this was an experience all its own. I wept for it and celebrated this time that led me to peace.

On February 20, 2012, I had written the following in my journal:

What is peace to me? Especially in a world where evil and unrest will continue. It means fearing not, especially not waking up in absolute terror in the middle of the night thinking that someone or something is about to kill me. It means not having anxiety attacks. It means being at peace with God . . . is that at the crux of this? It means being able to live in the moment and not have to check out with food or busyness or technology or shopping. It means being able to experience true joy as well as true sorrow because I am no longer numb with fear. It means being able to live authentically, fully revealing the image of God, fully participating in creation.

For almost forty years, fear had ruled my life. It took years and years of night terrors and interpersonal problems and a perfectionism that gripped me by the throat before I began to understand this. And when I had finally had enough, I prayed. I prayed desperate prayers that centered on one thing: peace. I wanted to be released from fear so I could live life from a place of peace. After months and even years passed, it seemed like God was ignoring my prayers. Now, I can look back and see the ways in which God persistently, faithfully, gently led me toward peace. Peace had always been there; I had only to release my hold on fear to receive it. The Academy showed me how to do that. Better still, it pointed me to the source of my peace. Our scripture passage points us toward a similar understanding.

Following the sorrow of the crucifixion, the disciples are stunned and thrilled to see Jesus alive. They realize they'll have an opportunity to spend more time with him. But after forty days Jesus informs them that the time has come for him to ascend to heaven. I imagine they begin to feel sad again, knowing they will miss this man who has meant so much to them and the world. But Jesus assures them they will not be alone. He will send his Holy Spirit to be a companion for them, constantly reminding them of Christ's deep love for them. Not only that, the Spirit will teach and mentor, helping them to remember his teaching and encouraging them to live out that teaching. In this life in the Spirit they will have peace, the peace that comes from God's love and leads right back to it, all the while calming, comforting, inspiring, and rejoicing. They are not losing Jesus; they are gaining peace.

❖

Stephen Colbert, a comedian who recently succeeded David Letterman as host of *Late Night*, had previously hosted *The Colbert Report* and also served as a cast member for *The Daily Show*. I never followed him too closely. That changed in November 2015 when he appeared on the cover of GQ magazine. In the featured interview, Colbert told the story of his father and two brothers who were killed in a plane crash in 1974; he was ten years old. A lifelong Catholic, Colbert described how the tragedy knocked him off center throughout his adolescence and young adult years; but ultimately, his faith redirected him to God, who had always been with him. Colbert holds a deep faith and has created a full life despite the trauma he experienced. But the interviewer and I were both startled when, referring to the tragedy, he said, "I love the thing that I most wish had not happened."

I can adopt this beautiful statement of faith for myself. Given my healing journey, I can say with confidence that I too love the thing I most wish had not happened. That's not to say I am glad the trauma happened. There is a difference. I wish it had not happened, full stop. But it did, and with what I've learned and experienced since then, I can now say that I love it. The molestation is part of my story and of who I am. It has shaped me. For so long, it defined me and surrounded me with fear. But it has led me to a fuller understanding of God's deep love for me and the ways I am called to share that deep love with others, particularly those who are in pain. I am now in a place of complete peace, with a life that is rich and fulfilling and resplendent. (This idea is similar to a concept known as Radical Acceptance. The resource list on pages 139–40 includes an article on this concept under the heading Trauma, PTSD, and Recovery.)

Accepting my trauma is not the same as saying God put the trauma in my life so I would learn these lessons; that's just another way of saying God causes evil, which is completely antithetical to what I believe about God. And, to be sure, many people who have rich, God-filled lives did not experience trauma; trauma isn't the only path to peace. My point is that I don't believe trauma has to be the end of the story. It is only one chapter of the book that is our lives. And it can lead to places of profound joy if we are willing to be still, speak our truth, and experience God's healing grace.

I pray that you too will find peace. It may take a while, and that's okay. Be gentle with yourself, knowing the peace of Jesus Christ is there for you to recognize and embrace when you are ready. Once you do, enjoy it. Revel in it. Be consumed by it. But do not keep it for yourself, because it is not yours to keep. True peace is meant to be shared. Indeed, when you experience peace, you will be compelled to share this gift with others. You won't be able to help yourself. You will want to support others in speaking their truths and healing their spirits so they too can splash about and delight in God's deep love. In this way, God's power will work in you to do infintely more than you could ask or imagine.

That's the gift of the Holy Spirit.

REFLECTION QUESTIONS

1. What does it mean to you that Jesus sends the Holy Spirit to offer peace in our lives?
2. How do you experience the presence of the Holy Spirit in your life?
3. Do you have a sense of God's peace? If so, how, when, where?
4. How do you cultivate a sense of peace in your life?
5. How do you feel about Stephen Colbert's statement? What would your statement of faith sound like?
6. Who is God calling you to be? How can you trust in God and "God's power to work in you to do infinitely more than you could ask or imagine"?
7. How can you bear witness to God's peace in the world?

PRAYER BEAD EXPERIENCE

Cross: God of love,

Invitatory bead: help me to experience your peace

Resurrection bead: by the power of your Son, Jesus Christ.

1st cruciform bead: Thank you for sending your Holy Spirit into the world so that I may be comforted and have peace.

Week beads, set 1: Use each bead to offer gratitude for God's Holy Spirit.

2nd cruciform bead: Help me to recognize the presence of the Holy Spirit in my life.

Week beads, set 2: Use each bead to consider the ways in which the Holy Spirit is present in your life.

3rd cruciform bead: Lead me to a place of peace in my life.

Week beads, set 3: Use each bead to ask God to lead you to a place of peace, taking time to note what peace will look, feel, and sound like.

4th cruciform bead: Help me to live into your calling for me so that I may be a witness to your peace in the world.

Week beads, set 4: Use each bead to consider who God is calling you to be and to ask for God's guidance to realize that calling.

Resurrection bead: In the name of Jesus Christ,

Invitatory bead: who offers his peace.

Cross: Amen.

Listening Focus

Grant me peace, Lord.

What Do You Notice?

What insights, feelings, memories, or other wisdom arose as you read the chapter material or completed the prayer bead experience? Whom can you share this with?

Take a minute to use your prayer beads to connect with your body. Sit quietly and breathe deeply with each bead. As you do, stay present in the moment, releasing any concerns, anxiety, or distractions. Embrace this place of stillness with God before you continue your journey.

WHOLENESS

After this I looked and there was a door that had been opened in heaven. The first voice that I had heard, which sounded like a trumpet, said to me, "Come up here, and I will show you what must take place after this." At once I was in a Spirit-inspired trance and I saw a throne in heaven, and someone was seated on the throne. Then I looked, and I heard the sound of many angels surrounding the throne, the living creatures, and the elders. They numbered in the millions—thousands upon thousands. They said in a loud voice, "Worthy is the slaughtered Lamb to receive power, wealth, wisdom, and might, and honor, glory, and blessing." And I heard every creature in heaven and on earth and under the earth and in the sea—I heard everything everywhere say, "Blessing, honor, glory, and power belong to the one seated on the throne and to the Lamb forever and always."

—Revelation 4:1-2; 5:11-13

Truth-telling

"So the book is about using prayer beads to heal from trauma. I want to explore how the beads can help address spiritual questions and share the pain with God."

Johnny, the Academy director, sat across the table from me. I was in Nashville to film a video with The Upper Room and was glad to have a chance to catch up with him. I hadn't seen him since graduating from The Academy the previous year.

"It's going to talk a lot about my time at The Academy and how The Academy model helped me in my healing. It will start with the need to speak your truth, then it will cover the various stages of healing; you know, grief, anger, shame, abandonment, etc. That will lead to forgiveness, love, peace ... "

"Wholeness," added Johnny.

I nodded my head vigorously, making it clear I had planned to include a chapter on wholeness.

Only, I hadn't. It hadn't even occurred to me.

"Absolutely," I said, not at all sure what I had to say on the subject.

Two hours later I was making the rounds through The Upper Room headquarters, stopping in to greet the people I knew. Sitting in Beth Richardson's office, I offered her a similar spiel about the book, describing how I thought prayer beads could help trauma survivors feel safe about encountering God.

"Oh, that sounds like EMDR," Beth noted. "It uses the senses to help people connect with their bodies and feelings. Studies have shown how effective it is for trauma survivors. My friend works with children who have been in abusive situations, and she says you can see them instantly relax when they use EMDR."

I'd heard of EMDR before. Indeed, Beth was the third or fourth person in the span of three months to tell me about EMDR and its use with trauma survivors. I took that as a sign that I needed to try it out. Since my time at The Academy, I had been doing really well. My prayer life was rich; I experienced gratitude daily, and I continued to feel a deep sense of God's love and peace. But those pesky night disturbances still hung around. Granted, they no longer terrified me, and they were much less frequent; but they were annoying and signaled that my body was still holding on to something.

Researching EMDR on the Internet, I learned that it stood for Eye Movement Desensitization and Reprocessing and was developed in the 1980s. The website went on to explain in this way:

> Eye movements (or other bilateral stimulation) are used during one part of the session. After the clinician has determined which memory to target first, he [or she] asks the client to hold different aspects of that event or thought in mind and to use his [or her] eyes to track the therapist's hand as it moves back and forth across the client's field of vision. As this happens, for reasons believed by a Harvard researcher to be connected with the biological mechanisms involved in Rapid Eye Movement (REM) sleep, internal associations arise and the clients begin to process the memory and disturbing

feelings. In successful EMDR therapy, the meaning of painful events is transformed on an emotional level. For instance, a rape victim shifts from feeling horror and self-disgust to holding the firm belief that, "I survived it and I am strong." Unlike talk therapy, the insights clients gain in EMDR result not so much from clinician interpretation, but from the client's own accelerated intellectual and emotional processes. The net effect is that clients conclude EMDR therapy feeling empowered by the very experiences that once debased them. Their wounds have not just closed, they have transformed. (http://www.emdr.com/what-is-emdr/)

The notion intrigued me. The website listed certified practitioners of EMDR. I found a therapist near me and scheduled an appointment. During my first session, Heather, my therapist, showed me the machine she would use: a small box that lay on the floor. Extending from it were two small wires that had pulsars on the end of them. Laying one in each of my hands, she explained that I could choose to feel the pulsars vibrate gently in my hands, back and forth, left to right. This was the tactile option. Alternatively, I could choose the visual option, which involved looking at the pulsars as a red light blinked, first left then right. Lastly, she offered an aural option: a set of headphones I could wear to listen to a soft sound played back and forth from one ear to the other. With each option, Heather would be able to control the back-and-forth speed from a low to a high frequency. I chose the tactile option, particularly because it allowed me to close my eyes during the session.

We spent the second session using the device to create a "safe space," a place I could go to in my head in the event our sessions got too intense. Heather invited me to visualize this safe space and to describe it in great detail. All the while, the pulsars vibrated slowly in my hands. I relaxed, swinging softly in my mountaintop hammock, my safe place. We moved through several cycles where I described the safe space in detail, each time allowing me to add new details to my safe space in order to make it more real. When I reported that my cat had shown up to join me in the hammock, Heather felt confident that I was ready to begin the hard work.

She asked, "What is the overall message of your night disturbances?"

"I made the wrong choice; therefore, I am going to be killed."

"Think about that message while you picture the scene of your molestation." She leaned down and turned the machine on. The pulsars vibrated rapidly in my hands. Left, right, left, right, left, right. I closed my

eyes and saw my seven-year-old self being led into the storage closet by the
bicycle guy. I felt fear, though it wasn't overwhelming. In my head I repeated,
"I made the wrong choice; therefore, I am going to be killed."

A few minutes later, I heard Heather say, "Take a deep breath and open
your eyes." I did so as she turned off the machine. "What did you notice?"
she asked.

"I just remembered crying and feeling terrified. I recalled certain
sensations, like the sound of his breathing."

"I want you to go with that thought and go back to that memory."

I closed my eyes. The pulsars began vibrating again. We did this two more
times. Each time I remembered or realized something new about the event.
By the fourth time, I noticed the bicycle guy was moving farther away from
me. I couldn't see him clearly.

"I think I'm not concentrating very well," I told her.

"No problem. That happens," she replied. "Just keep going."

I closed my eyes, picturing the guy. Wanting to stay focused, I looked
at him intently and repeated, "I am with you. I am with you. I am with
you." Instantly, the guy disappeared. In his place stood my mother, who was
reaching for me and saying, "I am with you. I am with you. I am with you."

"Oh, my God!" I said when Heather stopped the machine. I told her
what happened. She smiled.

"Go with that," she said.

I closed my eyes again. The pulsars vibrated left, right, left, right. I saw my
mother standing with me in front of the storage closet. She was holding me,
still repeating, "I am with you." But we weren't alone. The police had arrived,
and I watched as they led the bicycle guy away in handcuffs toward a group
of cop cars.

Heather looked pleased when I reported this. I was thrilled. I knew that
in just mere moments, I had been able to let go of the guy and the terror he'd
brought into my life. I'd also gotten the two things I'd needed most when I
was seven: comfort from my mom and justice.

"It sounds like you're doing well," said Heather. "To make sure there's not
anything else there to deal with, I want you to go back and repeat the original
message, 'I made the wrong choice; therefore, I am going to be killed.'"

I closed my eyes. Left, right, left, right, left, right. I saw the guy leading
me up the stairway and toward the storage closet, telling me to get in. But
instead of going in I began kicking and punching him. With everything I had

I screamed, "No! I trusted you and was willing to help you! But I didn't sign up for this!" Then I gave him one last good kick and ran away.

Kristie, my seven-year-old self, had just discovered her inner warrior. No one was going to hurt her anymore. She felt empowered, confident, free.

One last time, Heather asked me to close my eyes as she turned on the pulsars. With the vibration level on the same slow, gentle rhythm we had used when I was picturing my safe place, she said, "This time, I want you to repeat to yourself, 'I did the best I could.'"

I relaxed and repeated the phrase. As I did, I saw little Kristie. She—I— was smiling. And dancing.

I continued to meet Heather for a few more sessions to deal with other matters. We went from handling serious issues to addressing less traumatic events, instances in my life when I'd walked away feeling shame or anger. In every case, the EMDR machine did the trick, helping me transform past hurts into moments of great insight and healing.

As of this writing, the night disturbances have almost become a thing of the past. Granted, I still have one every now and then, particularly on stressful days. But they are a mere blip on the radar, and I see them now for what they are: a way for my body to release the stress of the day and remind me to do a better job of caring for myself. They no longer hold any sense of terror; the fear is completely gone.

Beth was spot on when she made the connection between EMDR and prayer beads. I shared this observation with Heather after one session, and asked if prayer beads could serve a similar function. "Absolutely," she responded. "You can use prayer beads. You might hold them with both hands so that you can touch one side of the set and then the other. Or you can pat your hands alternately on one leg or arm, then the next. The key is bilateral stimulation: right, left, right, left. Granted, it's important to do this with a trained practitioner until you get the EMDR concept; but now that you've experienced it, you can use these techniques in situations where you need help to calm down or to process an event or feeling right away."

I left this experience with a deeper sense of the mystery and miracle of our bodies. I find it humbling to see what they do on a daily basis to keep us going: how our brains process the millions of bits of information that come to us each day so that we can learn and react and function; how our muscles and bones work together to enable us to move about and participate in the world; and how our senses allow us to engage in and enjoy God's astounding creation. In his book *Now and Then*, Frederick Buechner writes, "Listen to your life. See it for the fathomless mystery that it is. In the boredom and pain of it no less than in the excitement and gladness: touch, taste, smell your way to the holy and hidden heart of it because in the last analysis all moments are key moments, and life itself is grace" (p. 87). We are such a miracle!

But when you consider what our bodies do for us during and after trauma, that is what I find truly stunning. I consider my brain's reaction when it realized I was in trouble and something bad was about to happen; how my heart, mind, and body instantly began to work together to get me through the event; how my brain worked to help me cope with the aftermath and go from day to day; how my body absorbed the feelings and memories and held them until I could safely process them; and how my heart, mind, and body have worked together over recent years to help me release, understand, and move on. Traumatic events affect the whole of our being: our minds, hearts, bodies, and spirits. The journey toward wholeness, then, comes in paying attention to and healing all these aspects of ourselves.

And it is a journey. Everything is a journey, but healing in particular is a journey. As Paul taught me, it's a process. And as I'm learning, it is a lifelong process. Sitting here today writing the end of this book, I look back on the healing that has occurred in my life and see it for the fantastic miracle that it is. But, as they say, my work here is not done. I still have issues to work on and lessons to learn and ways to grow toward wholeness. Growing in faith and wisdom will take a lifetime, as will healing from trauma. But if I pay attention, every day I will see new ways in which God is present in my life, calling me toward perfection. It's a process that I've learned to trust.

If Daniel 10:19 summarizes my entire theology, Revelation 4 and 5 illustrate the purpose of the journey and what this is all about. In these chapters we see a vision of all creation—all of it—coming together to praise God at the end of days. As one, we bow before Jesus Christ to exalt him. Our praise is effusive: we shout, play instruments, dance, and celebrate. But like my grief dreams when I couldn't cry hard enough, in this scene we cannot praise loudly enough. There are not enough words to praise God, and so we repeat ourselves, saying over and over,

> "Holy, holy, holy is the Lord God Almighty,
> who was and is and is coming" (4:8).

And we cry,
"Blessing, honor, glory, and power
belong to the one seated on the throne" (5:13).

And we dance and sing and laugh and skip. It is what we've got, all that we have, and we give it all in joyful offering.

We journey toward wholeness so that one day we can join together and worship the Creator, offering up every last bit of our lives: the wonders and mysteries, the ups and downs, the celebrations and traumas, the pain and the healing. Because God was in all of it and revealed in all of it.

May your journey continue, knowing that God's deep love is with you every second, guiding you, healing you, redeeming you, calling you to peace. Calling you to wholeness.

Because that is your true story.

REFLECTION QUESTIONS

1. Do you agree that healing is a lifelong process? Why or why not?
2. How do you feel at this point in your healing journey?
3. How and where have you seen God in your healing journey?
4. Focusing on your heart, mind, body, and soul, what differences do you see in yourself since beginning this study?
5. What are the next steps in your healing process? What support do you need as you continue to heal?
6. What does wholeness mean to you?
7. How can you pay attention and see God in your healing journey?

Prayer Bead Experience

Cross: God of wholeness,

Invitatory bead: help me to experience wholeness

Resurrection bead: by the power of your Son, Jesus Christ.

1st cruciform bead: Illuminate the ways in which you have helped me in my healing.

Week beads, set 1: Use each bead to reflect on your journey so far and see the signs of God's presence.

2nd cruciform bead: I recognize this is a lifelong journey; help me to trust you.

Week beads, set 2: Use each bead to acknowledge that healing is a journey and to practice trusting God.

3rd cruciform bead: Help me to know the next steps in my journey.

Week beads, set 3: Use each bead to consider the next steps in your healing journey.

4th cruciform bead: Be present for me each step of my journey.

Week beads, set 4: Use each bead to pray for knowledge of God's presence and to practice paying attention.

Resurrection bead: In the name of Jesus Christ,

Invitatory bead: the Lord God Almighty.

Cross: Amen.

Listening Focus

God calls me to wholeness.

What Do You Notice?

What insights, feelings, memories, or other wisdom arose as you read the chapter material or completed the prayer bead experience? Whom can you share this with?

Take a minute to use your prayer beads to connect with your body. Sit quietly and breathe deeply with each bead. As you do, stay present in the moment, releasing any concerns, anxiety, or distractions. Embrace this place of stillness with God before you continue in your journey.

One Last Thing . . .

In the months I spent writing this book, I was in the process of downsizing. I wanted fewer possessions, more space, less to dust, greater opportunities to connect with God. One day I was clearing out a collection of slides I had inherited from my grandfather, an avid photographer. Moving quickly, I lifted each one up to the light, determining which to keep, which to discard, throwing them into various piles. Until I came to one. I held it up to the light, studying it long and hard. Stunned, I realized I was looking at a photo of Creel Chapel at Camp Sumatanga. No one is in the photo; my grandfather must have taken it merely to appreciate the beauty of this sacred place. The date on the back of the slide is November 1966. I was in my mother's womb.

Even before I was born, God was preparing this place for a time of great healing.

Told you this was a love story.

Ralph C. Corrie

Praise be to God, who was, is, and always will be
. . . abiding with us, loving us, healing us.

WRITE YOUR OWN DEVOTION

As you grow in your journey and comfort level with prayer beads I invite you to write your own prayer bead devotion. Doing so offers a wonderful opportunity to consider how you want to pray: What do you want to ponder, to share with or hear from God? It also offers another tool for your healing journey as you enter new phases of your healing. You might write one devotion as you work to develop the courage to speak your truth, another as you delve into your grief or anger, another to celebrate a new sense of peace in your life. The time of writing can be a prayer in and of itself.

I offer this devotion I wrote to honor my healing journey as an example.

Cross: God of deep love,
Invitatory bead: you have known and loved me even before I was born.
Resurrection bead: I am yours.
1st cruciform bead: I spoke my truth, and you listened.
Week beads, set 1: I use each bead to reflect on the journey toward speaking my truth and recognizing the many ways in which God listened and responded.
2nd cruciform bead: I offered my spirit, broken and desolate, and you healed me.
Week beads, set 2: I use each bead to remember the ways in which God offered healing to me.
3rd cruciform bead: For so long I prayered desperately for peace; now, I live in your peace.
Week beads, set 3: I use each bead to to offer gratitude for God's peace in my life.
4th cruciform bead: Guide me in my continued journey toward wholeness.
Week beads, set 4: I use each bead to pray for God's help in my lifelong path toward wholeness.
Resurrection bead: In the name of your Son, Jesus Christ,
Invitatory bead: the full embodiment of your deep love.
Cross: Amen.

Listening Focus

I live in peace.

I have provided a template below; however, feel free to create your own. As always, there is no wrong way to pray. No matter what, you will be blessed in your desire to connect with God.

Your Own Devotion

Cross:

Invitatory bead:

Resurrection bead:

1st cruciform bead:

Week beads, set 1:

2nd cruciform bead:

Week beads, set 2:

3rd cruciform bead:

Week beads, set 3:

4th cruciform bead:

Week beads, set 4:

Resurrection bead:

Invitatory bead:

Cross: Amen.

LEADER'S GUIDE

Given the subject matter of this book, I strongly encourage you to invite a therapist, spiritual director, or pastor to help lead this study. It is possible the material will trigger particular emotions or memories for some participants, making it critical to have trained professionals available to provide appropriate support. They can also assist in facilitating the group to promote balanced participation from all members.

I have designed this book to be a sixteen-week Bible study, using the following suggested schedule:

- One week for welcome, introduction, and study overview
- One week for making prayer beads
- Three weeks on Speaking Your Truth
- Five weeks on Healing Your Spirit
- Six weeks on Experiencing God's Peace with wrap-up and next steps

However, it will be important to emphasize that participants' healing will, in all likelihood, take longer than sixteen weeks. Indeed, this book chronicles a multiyear journey for me. Encourage group members to use this book and your group as a guide and an opportunity to begin to explore their story. Give them permission to heal in their own time.

One hour is enough time for each meeting, with the exception of the bead-making session, which may require one and a half to two hours. If possible, encourage participants to purchase the book and read the Introduction prior to the first meeting.

As the study leader, plan to arrive early to prepare the room. I recommend arranging chairs around a table so that group members face one another. This arrangement will facilitate dialogue as well as allow space for books, prayer beads, and notes. If a table is not available, arrange chairs in a circle.

I would also encourage you to consider ways to create a prayerful mood in the meeting room. Perhaps you can light a candle and play soft instrumental music in the background as members arrive or set up a small worship center with a cross and/or Bible. There is no need to make this complicated; simple settings often lend themselves to a spirit of prayer.

INTRODUCTORY MEETING

Since this will be the first time for the group to meet, take time to welcome each participant. Then, allow each person to introduce himself or herself. As part of the introductions, invite participants to

- share, if they feel comfortable, a brief summary of what drew them to this study.
- share whether they have used prayer beads before.
- indicate what they hope to receive from this study.

Next, orient the group members to the study. Ask if anyone had specific questions about the Introduction. Then review the study outline: The study takes place over sixteen weeks. The second week the group will meet to make prayer beads. Emphasize that even if they have a set of prayer beads or have made them previously, participants are encouraged to make a set of prayer beads with this group to help build group cohesion for the study. The second week also provides a good opportunity to review A Guide to Using Prayer Beads, particularly if group members are unfamiliar with this practice and its history.

The next three weeks will focus on the first section of the book, Speaking Your Truth, offering an opportunity for participants to accept God's invitation to healing, to learn to be still with God, and to begin to share their story. Following this, the group will spend five weeks on the section Healing Your Spirit. During this time, participants will have the opportunity to explore various elements of their trauma and its impact. The final six weeks will look at Experiencing God's Peace. Here, participants will explore the different elements of healing and living into God's peace and wholeness.

Each week includes a scripture passage, Truth-Telling, Reflection Questions, Prayer Bead Experience, and Listening Focus. The end of each chapter features a time to check in and notice what feelings, thoughts, and memories have come up as a result of the material. Participants are then invited to consider with whom they will share these thoughts and feelings and then use the prayer beads to connect with the body before moving on.

Encourage the participants to do the following:

- take 30–45 minutes each week to read the assigned scripture and Truth-Telling; review the Reflection Questions.
- use a journal to write down any additional questions, thoughts, and/or feelings they may have and bring them to the study meetings;
- spend at least five minutes each day practicing the Prayer Bead Experience and/or Listening Focus; and
- spend at least five to ten minutes once a week completing the What Did You Notice? section and prayer bead exercise.

Assure the participants that there are no right or wrong ways to use prayer beads. This study introduces people to a variety of ways to use beads in prayer and gives participants an opportunity to experiment, using the Prayer Bead Experiences. Some of the experiences may be more comfortable or compelling than others, and that is okay. The experiences may inspire participants to come up with their own ways of using beads in prayer. Ultimately, the beads are intended to help people draw closer to God. Hopefully, the beads will help them gain a certain comfort level with prayer, experience God in a new way, feel more connected to God, and learn to "listen" to God.

In closing, offer the following prayer:

Loving God, we come to you with our pain and brokenness. Whether this pain be recent or from long ago, we arrive with our individual stories and our particular feelings. We may be tired, fearful, angry, full of shame, or about to give up.

And yet, we are hopeful. We hope you are there to receive our pain, hear our stories, offer comfort, and bring us to a place of healing. We hope we can open ourselves up long enough to recognize your presence. We hope we can be healed and made whole. We hope.

And so we pray you will bless our time together. Be in our midst and in our hearts as we move through this study, building trust with you, ourselves, and one another, trusting that no matter what has happened in our lives, you love us deeply. Amen.

Making Prayer Beads

If you plan to make prayer beads with your group, I recommend you set aside about one or one and one-half hours.

A supply list, along with complete instructions and a video, can be found at http://prayerworksstudio.com/prayer-beads/make-your-own/. You will need to determine ahead of time whether to provide the supplies for group members and, if so, whether to charge a materials fee to cover the costs. If so, I encourage you to notify group members of the cost ahead of time. Otherwise, you may provide a supply list and encourage participants to bring their own supplies. To maximize your time, review the instructions or watch the instructional video prior to the bead-making session.

Even better, by making a set of prayer beads in advance you ensure your own preparation to lead group members through this activity and have a sample set to show them. You will serve as their inspiration!

At the end of your bead-making time, gather the group members and invite them to hold the prayer beads they have just made. Then pray the following blessing:

> Creator God, you love us enough to call us into your presence through prayer and for that we give thanks.
>
> We thank you for the many ways in which we can connect with you, including through the use of prayer beads.
>
> We ask your blessing upon these beads. May they remind us of your loving presence, draw us into prayer, focus our time with you, and help us to listen to what you have to say to us. May these beads be useful in our healing journey. We pray this in Jesus' name. Amen.

Weekly Format

Opening

When all participants arrive and find a seat, take a moment to help everyone transition from the noise and rush of daily life to this time of reflection and discussion. Encourage participants to hold their prayer beads, close their eyes, and take three deep breaths. This does not have to be formal; let it be an opportunity to relax and be still in God's presence.

Pray the week's Prayer Bead Experience together

If participants feel comfortable doing so, invite one participant to be the leader for the day. The leader will read the Prayer Bead Experience out loud while participants hold their prayer beads and follow along with each bead. When the leader comes to the cruciform bead, he or she will read the prayer for that bead aloud, then allow time for silence as the participants pray silently while fingering each of the week beads. After providing a sufficient amount of time for the participants to pray with all week beads (about one minute), the leader will read the prayer for the next cruciform bead out loud. Continue in this way through the conclusion of the prayer. Another option comes in inviting the group to use the Listening Focus—rather than the devotion—to open the study.

Read the week's scripture passage aloud

After a volunteer reads the scripture aloud, invite the group members to take a moment for prayerful consideration of the scripture, or you may say, "The word of God for the people of God." They would respond by saying, "Thanks be to God." Then invite participants to state aloud any thoughts or insights they received while listening.

Reflect on the week's Truth-Telling

Invite participants to spend a few minutes reflecting on the Truth-Telling section. You may prompt them with questions such as, "What was meaningful for you in this chapter?" or "What did you notice in yourself as you read this chapter?"

Review the Reflection Questions

You may choose to take each question in order. Read it aloud and allow time for the group members' responses. Another option is to invite group members to speak about the questions they found most thought-provoking.

You may not have the answers to all the questions. That is okay. Do the best you can and feel free to invite responses from others in the group. If you have the opportunity, consider reviewing other resources that relate to a particular chapter using the list provided in the Resources section (page 139). If you do not know the answer to a question, invite group members to do additional research on their own.

The challenge in working with groups comes in finding a balance between the extroverts and the introverts. Inevitably, you will have members who are talkative and feel comfortable speaking up while others are shy and quiet. It is important to create an environment in which every participant feels encouraged and comfortable to share if he or she chooses without putting undue pressure on those who prefer to remain silent. If you find yourself leading a group that is unusually quiet, experiment with ways of encouraging each member to participate without putting him or her on the spot.

Share observations from the Prayer Bead Experience

Review one or all of the questions below or encourage participants to share thoughts about the experience.

- How did the experience assist in your healing journey?
- How did the experience help in your understanding of using prayer beads as a healing tool?
- How did the experience aid your understanding of connecting and communicating with God?

What Did You Notice?

Invite any group members who are willing to share insights, feelings, memories, or other wisdom that the chapter's reading, questions, or prayer bead experience may have prompted. Whether anyone shares or not, encourage participants to do this exercise each week. In addition, use this time to reinforce the need for support people with whom they can share their insights.

Closing

Choose one of the following options:

Invite a participant to lead the group through a closing prayer.

Invite the group members to use their beads to take deep breaths, as suggested in the What Did You Notice? section of the chapter.

FINAL MEETING

You may want to set aside one and one-half hours for the final meeting. This gives sufficient time to review the chapter material and encourage participants to consider their next steps. The study may help participants to identify issues or areas for continued focus after the study. Help them consider how to go about addressing these issues or areas (such as meeting with a therapist or pastor, signing up for a yoga class, etc.). In addition, encourage group members to consider sources of support following the study. Finally, take time to celebrate their journey to this point, and encourage them in their continued healing.

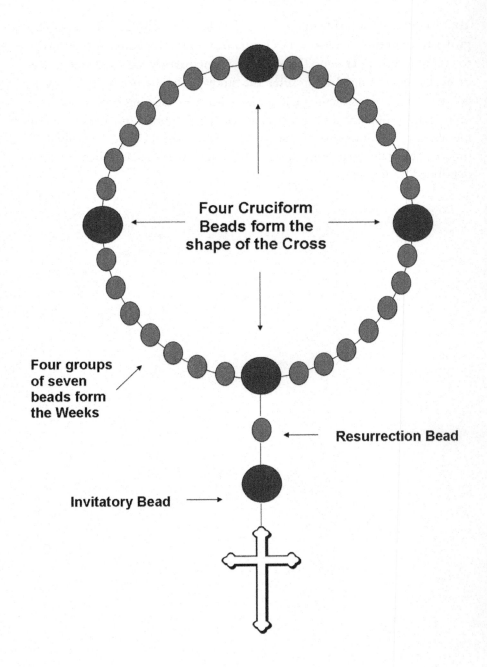

Four Cruciform
Beads form the
shape of the Cross

Four groups
of seven
beads form
the Weeks

Resurrection Bead

Invitatory Bead

A GUIDE TO USING
PRAYER BEADS

You are embarking on a journey that will introduce you to a new way of connecting with God. Protestant prayer beads are a prayer tool that can help you experience God's presence, increase your focus and comfort level in prayer, and be still and know God's love for you.

While many types of prayer beads exist, I designed the devotions in this book for use with Protestant prayer beads. Many Protestants are unfamiliar with this form of prayer beads; they are generally more familiar with the beads used by Catholics to pray the rosary. The two forms of prayer beads certainly have some common history, both evolving as a way for Christians to "pray continually" (1 Thess. 5:17). The rosary is at least one thousand years old, but a group of Episcopalians in Texas developed Protestant prayer beads in the 1980s. The group wanted to reclaim ancient prayer practices, and after meeting for a period of time they created the "Anglican rosary," a format of prayer beads for Protestant use.

Sixty beads make up the rosary; Protestant prayer beads are made up of a cross or other pendant and thirty-three or more beads. One large bead, called the "invitatory" bead, reminds us that God invites us to a time of prayer. We use this bead to begin our prayer, much like churches employ a call to worship to begin a church service.

In addition to the large invitatory bead, we find four more large beads. When we splay out a set of Protestant prayer beads, these beads form the four points of a cross and thus are called "cruciform" beads. Beyond representing the points of the cross, the number 4 reminds us of the four Gospels, the four seasons of the year, the four parts of our day (morning, afternoon, evening, and night), and the four directions (north, south, east, and west).

Between each of the cruciform beads is a set of seven smaller beads. Because a week has seven days, these beads are called "week" beads. Like the number 4, the number 7 has bountiful meaning for Christians:

- The church calendar consists of seven seasons (Advent, Christmas, Epiphany, Lent, Easter, Pentecost, and Ordinary Time).
- Genesis tells us there were seven days of Creation; on the seventh day God rested, calling us to keep it holy;
- the number 7 shows up often in the book of Revelation, including John's note that his letter is addressed to the "seven churches" (1:4);
- both Jews and Christians believe the number 7 symbolizes spiritual perfection. When we add together the one invitatory bead, the four cruciform beads, and the twenty-eight week beads, we get a total of thirty-three beads. (See diagram on page 134.) The group that developed this format appreciated this number since it represented Jesus' life on earth for thirty-three years.

For the first year I chose to use that number of beads. However, over time I began to desire some representation of the fact that Christ still lives today, particularly since the Resurrection is the hallmark of the Christian faith. So I added one more bead, positioning it between the invitatory bead and the bottom cruciform bead. I call it the "resurrection" bead and use it in my prayers to focus on Christ's gift to us of eternal life. Adding this bead makes the total number of beads thirty-four. However, I still tell people that Protestant prayer beads are comprised of thirty-three beads, which represent Jesus' life and ministry on earth—plus one bead to represent his resurrection.

This study will focus on the Protestant prayer bead format of thirty-four beads; however, you may design your own format as I did and modify the devotions accordingly. Since this is your prayer tool, it should be meaningful for you and your time with the Lord.

Like the rosary, Protestant prayer beads offer various benefits to prayer: They enhance focus, offer a way of being still, and serve as a sign of God's presence. But whereas the rosary has a formula for prayers to be said with each bead, Protestant prayer beads do not. This means you can use them in any way that feels comfortable to you and even experiment with different ways of using them. Consider this a wonderful opportunity to explore new ways of being—and healing—with God.

Acknowledgments

One of the greatest gifts to arise from your healing journey is the community that it creates. It is a vibrant, eclectic mix of folks who have always been with you and folks who joined in step with you at points along the way. I am deeply grateful for my community, particularly as the members helped me write this book. Who knew the value this writing process would have in my continued healing? Well, they did, of course. Deep love goes to the following:

The Academy for Spiritual Formation, which taught me to be still and pay attention, leading to the most profound healing experience of my life. Thanks to Johnny Sears; the #34 leadership team: Linda Beasley, Irene Brownlee, Blake Kendrick, Pat Luna, Kathy Norberg, and Robbins Sims; the #34 participants; Donna Bryant; Paul Bradford (and Albert); and, most especially, the members of The Almond Joys—my #34 covenant group: Horace Allen, Steve Cooper, Janet Harman, Lana Johnson, Amy Love, and Nell Sims.

My mom, who has offered the deepest of loves my entire life and who shared this journey with me each step of the way.

Max and Matthew, my husband and son, whose love and presence in my life are by far the surest signs of God's deep love for me. You are my delight. You sacrificed the most so that I could tell this tale. I will never be able to express the depth of my gratitude and love for you.

Jackie, my sister. You have loved me, worked with me, challenged me, and made me laugh along this journey. That you are (surprise!) a member of my family is one of life's greatest gifts.

Mike Selleck and the North Georgia Conference of The United Methodist Church; Barbara Sponberg and my parents, whose financial contributions allowed me to attend The Academy for Spiritual Formation.

CeCe Nickolich, my spiritual director. You were one of the first to hear my prayer for peace. Since then, you have steadily pointed to glimpses of peace until, together, we could articulate the complete picture.

Stacey Kitchens and Heather Kotler, the therapists who guided me on this journey.

Eva Young, who created the perfect environment in which to receive a healing vision.

Cyndi McDonald, who, through our biweekly Monastery meetings and a single tattoo adventure, taught me about *hesed* and offered holy communion on a variety of levels.

Thayer Manis, my longtime friend and fellow sojourner who has loved and taught me much. Your gift of prayer beads (black to symbolize God's mystery) remains one of my all-time favorites.

The soldiers and staff of the Functional Recovery Program at Eisenhower Army Medical Center, Fort Gordon, Georgia, who have shared their pain, listened to mine, made prayer beads, and offered profound insights into the kingdom of God.

The therapists, spiritual directors, pastors, fellow survivors, and friends who reviewed and provided invaluable feedback on the draft, including Vance Armor, Steve Cooper, Phil Gable, Lana Johnson, Amy Love, Thayer Manis, CeCe Nickolich, Kathy Norberg, Dalton Rushing, Stacey Rushing, Angela Schaffner, Johnny Sears, Nell Sims, and Tamara T.

Treah Caldwell, a trauma therapist who spent several sacred hours with me on the patio of Ria's Bluebird, educating me further about PTSD and recovery and inspiring key changes to the book's format. Dr. Angela Schaffner, a licensed psychologist, also helped shape this book.

Rita Collet, my editor. After three books together, we have become a team. I continue to love and appreciate your way with words—humorous, literary, and otherwise.

Fans and customers of Prayerworks Studio, whose support and stories of healing made tangible through prayer beads were profound, inspiring, and enlightening.

The members of Inman Park United Methodist Church, who welcomed me and my family into their lives and onto their porches, all the while cheering me on in this venture.

The monks and staff of the Monastery of the Holy Spirit, who offered grace-filled hospitality and the perfect setting as I prayerfully began work on this book.

The staff of Proof Bakeshop, who allowed me to camp out at their tables, tolerated my custom orders, and kept my cup overflowing with London Fogs as I completed work on the book.

Most especially, to the God of hope and healing. Really, there are no words. Praise you, praise you, praise you!

MY FAVORITE APPS, BOOKS, AND OTHER RESOURCES

Being Still

calm.com (app and website)

Shame and Vulnerability

Brown, Brené. *Daring Greatly: How the Courage to Be Vulnerable Transforms the Way We Live, Love, Parent, and Lead*. New York: Avery, 2012.

————. "Brené Brown: The Power of Vulnerability." Online video clip. Tedx Houston. ted.com, June 2010. Web. 16 April 2016.

Spiritual Formation

Benson, Robert. *The Echo Within: Finding Your True Calling*. Colorado Springs: WaterBrook Press, 2009.

————. *Living Prayer*. New York: Tarcher, 1998.

Buechner, Frederick. *Now and Then: A Memoir of Vocation*. New York: HarperCollins, 1983.

Eslinger, Elise S. *Upper Room Worshipbook: Music and Liturgies for Spiritual Formation* (Nashville, Tenn.: Upper Room Books, 2000).

Evans, Rachel Held. *Searching for Sunday: Loving, Leaving, and Finding the Church*. Nashville, TN: Thomas Nelson, 2015.

Kynes, Will. "God's Grace in the Old Testament: Considering the Hesed of the Lord." *Knowing & Doing*. Summer 2010. C. S. Lewis Institute. Web. 20 May 2016.

Nouwen, Henri J. M. *Life of the Beloved: Spiritual Living in a Secular World*. New York: Crossroad Publishing Company, 2014.

Paintner, Christine Valters. *The Soul of a Pilgrim: Eight Practices for the Journey Within*. Notre Dame: Sorin Books, 2015.

Parsons, John J. "Psalm 23 in Hebrew." *Hebrew for Christians*. Parsons, John J. Web. 20 May 2016.

Vincent, Max O. "More Than You Can Imagine." January 24, 2016. Inman Park United Methodist Church. Web. 27 May 2016.

Wright, N. T. *Evil and the Justice of God*. Madison: InterVarsity Press, 2006.

Spiritual Healing

Clem, Dale. *Winds of Fury, Circles of Grace: A Healing Journey through Grief and Tragedy*. Sarasota, FL: Bardolf & Company, 2010.

Hillesum, Etty and Eva Hoffman. *A Life Interrupted* and *Letters from Westerbork*. New York: Henry Holt & Company, 1996.

Hudson, Trevor. *Hope Beyond Your Tears: Experiencing Christ's Healing Love*. Nashville, TN: Upper Room Books, 2012.

Lovell, Joel. "The Late, Great Stephen Colbert." GQ, November 2015. GQ Web. 24 May 2016.

Young, William P. *The Shack*. Newbury Park: Windblown Media, 2007.

Trauma, PTSD, and Recovery

EMDR: www.emdr.com

Hall, Karyn. "Radical Acceptance: Sometimes Problems Can't Be Solved," *Psychology Today*. 8 July 2012. Psychology Today Web. 11 August 2016.

Herman, Judith. *Trauma and Recovery: The Aftermath of Violence—from Domestic Abuse to Political Terror*. New York: Basic Books, 2015.

Longden, Eleanor. "Listening to Voices." *Scientific American Mind*. September/October 2013.

McClelland, Mac. *Irritable Hearts: A PTSD Love Story*. New York: Flatiron Books, 2015.

Morris, David J. *The Evil Hours: A Biography of Post-Traumatic Stress Disorder*. New York: First Mariner Books, 2016.

Van der Kolk, Bessel. *The Body Keeps the Score: Brain, Mind, and Body in the Healing of Trauma*. New York: Penguin Books, 2014.

Wood, David. "Veterans Find Comfort in Meditation Therapy." *The Huffington Post*. 20 February 2015. The Huffington Post Web. June 19 2016.

ABOUT THE AUTHOR

KRISTEN E. VINCENT is an award-winning author, speaker, and artisan whose passion is spiritual formation, including the use of prayer beads. She is the author of *A Bead and a Prayer: A Beginner's Guide to Protestant Prayer Beads*, and coauthor of *Another Bead, Another Prayer: Devotions for Use with Protestant Prayer Beads* (with Max Vincent). She travels frequently to lead retreats and workshops. Kristen is a graduate of Duke Divinity School and The Academy for Spiritual Formation (#34). She lives in Atlanta, Georgia, with her husband, Max, a United Methodist pastor, and their son, Matthew. Kristen loves words, the mountains, gatherings on her porch . . . and dark chocolate. She continues to make progress in her lifelong quest for the perfect chocolate mousse. You can learn more at www.prayerworksstudio.com.

For bonus content, go to
beadsofhealing.com

The Academy for Spiritual Formation® is an experience of disciplined Christian community emphasizing holistic spirituality—nurturing body, mind, and spirit. The program, a ministry of The Upper Room®, is ecumenical in nature and meant for all those who hunger for a deeper relationship with God, including both lay and clergy persons. Each Academy fosters spiritual rhythms—of study and prayer, silence and liturgy, solitude and relationship, rest and exercise. With offerings of both Two-Year and Five-Day models, Academy participants rediscover Christianity's rich spiritual heritage through worship, learning, and fellowship. The Academy's commitment to an authentic spirituality promotes balance, inner and outer peace, holy living and justice living—God's shalom.

Faculty trained in the wide breadth of Christian spirituality and practice provide content and guidance at each session of The Academy. Academy faculty presenters come from seminaries, monasteries, spiritual direction ministries, and pastoral ministries or other settings and are from a variety of traditions. Author Kristen Vincent graduated from Academy #34.

The Academy Recommends program seeks to highlight content that aligns with the Academy's mission to provide resources and settings where pilgrims encounter the teachings, sustaining practices, and rhythms that foster attentiveness to God's Spirit and therefore help spiritual leaders embody Christ's presence in the world.

The ACADEMY RECOMMENDS program seeks to highlight content that aligns with the Academy's mission to provide resources and settings where pilgrims encounter the teachings, sustaining practices, and rhythms that foster attentiveness to God's Spirit and therefore help spiritual leaders embody Christ's presence in the world.

academy.upperroom.org

CPSIA information can be obtained
at www.ICGtesting.com
Printed in the USA
BVOW06s1646260517
485244BV00006B/58/P